Pickleball  DATING

LOVE ON THE COURT

DR. ESRA OZ

INGI, LLC

Published by: INGI, LLC

www.esraozdenerol.com

www.datingfunnelforwomen.com

ABOUT THE BOOK

Welcome to the world of Pickleball Dating, where the thrill of the game meets the excitement of romance! **Pickleball Dating: Love on the Court** is designed for those who are not only passionate about pickleball but are also looking to explore the possibility of finding love through this dynamic sport. This book is a comprehensive guide designed for singles and couples who want to explore the exciting intersection of romance and the popular sport of pickleball. Whether you're a seasoned player or new to the game, this guide will provide you with insights, tips, and strategies for navigating the unique landscape of dating in the pickleball community.

Throughout the book, readers will find practical worksheets, checklists, and tips to help them apply the concepts discussed. From creating an ideal partner profile to planning memorable pickleball dates, these tools provide actionable steps to enhance the dating experience. Readers will learn to understand the game and its community, assess their dating goals, find local leagues and online communities. They'll explore the Pickleball Dating Funnel to create an ideal partner profile and attract compatible players, along with tips for flirting on the court.

The book offers insights on how to plan memorable dates, navigate challenges like competition and breakups, and maintain friendships afterward. Through real-life success stories, readers will find inspiration and valuable lessons from couples who met through pickleball. Emphasizing the importance of balancing love and sport, the book encourages readers to embrace the joy of romance within the game and grow together through teamwork and shared goals.

Pickleball Dating: Love on the Court is more than just a guide to dating; it's an invitation to embrace the joy of the game while forming meaningful connections. Whether you're a seasoned player or new to the sport, this book will inspire you to navigate the pickleball dating scene with confidence and enthusiasm, ultimately leading to fulfilling relationships that thrive both on and off the court.

ABOUT THE AUTHOR

Esra Oz, commonly known as Dr. Esra Oz, is an author, coach, and the creator of datingfunnelforwomen.com. She is the author of **"Pickleball Dating: Love on the Court"**. The fast-paced action of pickleball leads to unexpected love matches both on and off the court. Sparks will fly as hearts and paddles collide.

You can also join her social media community **"Dating Funnel for Women"** on Facebook and/or Instagram for tips on dating and how to create a dating funnel, a simplistic dating approach, going on multiple dates and filtering out the high-value man, who is offering you the solidity, maturity, and adulthood you need for life partnership.

For more tips on how to date with more intention and less stress, listen to her podcast **"Dating Funnel for Women"** on Spotify and Apple Podcast. She also offers live group coaching on a rotating schedule and 1:1 coaching. Check out the website www.datingfunnelforwomen.com to see when the next session begins, explore the master class, and download a dating funnel blueprint as a reference for your dating journey and follow her on Instagram **@datingfunnelforwomen.**

Table of Contents

Chapter 1

Understanding Pickleball and Its Community

What is pickleball?

Pickleball is a fun, fast-paced racquet sport that combines elements of tennis, badminton, and table tennis. Played on a court similar to a doubles badminton court, it uses a net and a unique paddle to hit a perforated plastic ball back and forth. The game can be played as singles or doubles, making it versatile for different group sizes and skill levels.

Originating in the mid-1960s, pickleball has gained immense popularity, particularly among adults, due to its accessibility and the relatively low-impact nature of the game. It offers a great cardiovascular workout while being easy to learn, making it ideal for players of all ages. With its quirky name and friendly vibe, pickleball has created a unique community that values both competition and camaraderie.

The Playful Origins Behind Pickleball's Quirky Name

Pickleball got its quirky name from a playful combination of circumstances. The most popular story is that the game's inventors, Joel Pritchard, Bill Bell, and Barney McCallum, named it after Pritchard's family dog, "Pickles." According to this tale, Pickles would often chase after the ball during their early games, so they decided to name the game after their mischievous pet. However, another version suggests that the name "pickleball" actually came from a rowing term "pickle boat," which refers to a crew made up of leftover rowers from different teams. Since pickleball was created using a mix of elements from other sports (tennis, badminton, and ping-pong), this could have been an inspiration. While both stories circulate, the dog version is often the most widely embraced!

The Social Aspects of Pickleball

One of the standout features of pickleball is its strong social component. The sport encourages interaction and fosters relationships, making it a perfect avenue for meeting new people, including potential romantic partners. Many players form lasting friendships through shared games, tournaments, and community events.

Inclusive Environment: Pickleball is known for its welcoming atmosphere, where players of all skill levels come together to learn, play, and enjoy the game. This inclusivity helps break down social barriers, making it easier to strike up conversations and form connections.

Community Events: Many pickleball clubs host social events, clinics, and mixers that allow players to interact outside of regular play. These events can serve as excellent opportunities for dating, as they create a relaxed setting for getting to know fellow players.

Friendly Competition: The competitive nature of the game can also enhance social bonds. Friendly rivalries often develop, leading to playful banter and an engaging atmosphere. This shared experience can create a sense of camaraderie that translates into personal connections off the court.

Building Connections on the Court

Building connections through pickleball requires both intention and effort. Here are some tips to help you navigate the social landscape of the sport:

Join a Local Club: Becoming a member of a pickleball club or league is one of the best ways to meet new people. Attend regular play sessions and community events to immerse yourself in the local pickleball culture.

Participate in Group Play: Engaging in group play sessions allows for more social interaction than playing alone. Rotate partners during games to maximize the number of people you meet and establish connections.

Volunteer for Events: Many pickleball clubs organize tournaments and events that rely on volunteers. Getting involved not only supports the community but also places you in situations where you can meet and connect with other players.

Be Open and Approachable: A friendly demeanor can go a long way in fostering connections. Smile, make eye contact, and initiate conversations with fellow players. Sharing your enthusiasm for the game can make you more relatable and inviting.

Use Social Media: Many pickleball communities have online groups where players can connect, share tips, and arrange games. Engaging with these platforms can help you stay updated on local events and expand your network.

In conclusion, understanding the nature of pickleball and its community lays the foundation for building meaningful connections, both on and off the court. By immersing yourself in the sport and embracing its social aspects, you can enhance your pickleball experience while opening the door to new romantic possibilities.

Chapter 2

The Essentials of Pickleball Gear and Courts

Pickleball has quickly become one of the fastest-growing sports in the world, with its simple equipment and accessible gameplay drawing players from all walks of life. Though easy to pick up, understanding the nuances of the ball, paddles, and court layout can help elevate your game. In this chapter, we'll break down the essential components of pickleball, including the ball, the paddles, and the court dimensions and types.

The Pickleball: Small but Mighty

The pickleball itself may look unassuming, but its design is crucial to the sport's gameplay. A pickleball is a lightweight, perforated plastic ball that resembles a wiffle ball, with strategically placed holes that allow for controlled flight and less wind resistance. Standard pickleballs are 2.87 to 2.97 inches in diameter and weigh between 0.78 to 0.935 ounces. This small but mighty ball is engineered for accuracy and balance, making it perfect for the fast-paced rallies that pickleball is known for.

There are two main types of pickleballs, which vary slightly depending on where you play:

Outdoor Balls: Typically, outdoor pickleballs have larger and fewer holes (around 40) to handle wind and rougher court surfaces. These balls are generally harder, making them more durable for outdoor play, but they also bounce higher and are slightly faster.

Indoor Balls: Indoor pickleballs have smaller and more holes (around 26), which make them easier to control. They are lighter and softer, designed for the smooth indoor court surfaces that minimize wear and tear on the ball. Indoor balls tend to have a more controlled bounce and slower gameplay.

The Paddle: Finding the Perfect Fit

Pickleball paddles are a key element of the sport, with a wide range of materials, shapes, and sizes available. Unlike traditional tennis rackets, pickleball paddles are solid and flat. The size of a standard pickleball paddle is regulated, and it cannot exceed 24 inches in total length and width (typically 16 inches in length and 8 inches in width). The weight of a pickleball paddle can range from 6 to 14 ounces, which greatly affects its performance.

Materials and Types of Paddles

Paddles are typically made from a combination of materials, with three main types being popular today:

Wooden Paddles: These are the heaviest type of paddles, often used by beginners or in recreational play due to their durability and affordability. However, they can be cumbersome for more advanced players who value agility.

Composite Paddles: Made from a combination of materials like fiberglass or carbon fiber, composite paddles are a popular choice for intermediate players. They offer a great balance of weight, power, and control. These paddles often have a core made from polymer, aluminum, or Nomex, which influences their performance.

Graphite Paddles: The lightest and most advanced option, graphite paddles are favored by professionals. They offer superior control and power, and the lightweight nature allows players to react quickly during fast exchanges. The graphite face provides a smooth, responsive surface for striking the ball with precision.

What Makes a Good Paddle?

A good pickleball paddle balances control, power, and weight to match the player's style of play. There are a few factors to consider when choosing the right paddle:

Weight: Heavier paddles (8-14 ounces) provide more power, making it easier to drive the ball with less effort. However, they can be tiring for long games or defensive players. Lighter paddles

(6-8 ounces) offer better control and quicker reaction times but may lack power.

Grip Size: A paddle's grip size should match the player's hand size for comfort and maneuverability. Standard grips range from 4 to 4.5 inches in circumference.

Core Material: The paddle's core material (polymer, aluminum, or Nomex) affects its durability and performance. Polymer cores provide the most softness and control, while Nomex is harder and delivers more power.

The Court: Dimensions and Types

Pickleball courts are standardized, making them easy to set up and play in different locations. A pickleball court measures 20 feet wide and 44 feet long for both singles and doubles play, which is about the same size as a badminton court. The court is divided into several key sections:

Non-Volley Zone (Kitchen): This is the 7-foot area on both sides of the net where players are not allowed to volley the ball. Mastering the kitchen line is essential to becoming a good pickleball player.

Service Areas: The remaining sections of the court are divided into left and right service areas, each measuring 15 feet long by 10 feet wide. Serves must land in the diagonal service area on the opponent's side.

Court Surface Types

Pickleball can be played on a variety of surfaces, each offering a slightly different experience:

Outdoor Hard Courts: Typically made from asphalt or concrete and often shared with tennis courts, these surfaces are fast and can cause the ball to bounce higher. Outdoor courts are exposed to weather elements, which can affect ball control, especially in windy conditions.

Indoor Courts: Indoor courts are usually made from wood or synthetic surfaces, offering a smoother, more controlled playing experience. These courts tend to favor softer, indoor balls and provide consistent bounce due to the lack of outdoor elements.

Temporary or Portable Courts: Many pickleball players set up temporary courts in multi-purpose gyms or even on driveways and cul-de-sacs using portable nets and court markers. These are great for casual play or practice but may not offer the same consistency as permanent courts.

Differences Between Outdoor and Indoor Courts

While the court dimensions remain the same, the surface and environment impact gameplay significantly. Outdoor courts tend to be faster, with harder surfaces and wind playing a major role in the direction and speed of the ball. Indoor courts provide a more controlled environment, making for slower, more strategic games.

The ball, paddles, and court are all integral parts of the pickleball experience. From the lightweight, perforated pickleball itself to the various types of paddles and surfaces, every aspect plays a role in how the game unfolds. Whether you're playing on a smooth indoor court or an outdoor hard court, mastering your equipment and understanding the court layout will help you become a more well-rounded player.

Chapter 3

Using Social Media and Apps for Pickleball Dating

In today's digital age, social media and dating apps provide unique opportunities to connect with fellow pickleball enthusiasts. Using social media and dating apps to connect with fellow pickleball players opens up a world of possibilities for dating and friendship. By highlighting your love for the game, engaging in relevant communities, and approaching online conversations thoughtfully, you can create meaningful connections that extend beyond the court. Embrace the digital landscape to enhance your pickleball dating journey and have fun along the way!

This chapter explores how to leverage these platforms to enhance your pickleball dating experience.

Finding Local Pickleball Groups and Players

Join Pickleball-Specific Groups: Platforms like Facebook host numerous groups dedicated to pickleball. Search for local or regional groups where players gather to share tips, organize games, and post about upcoming events. Engaging in these groups allows you to meet potential dates who share your passion for the sport.

Follow Pickleball Influencers: Many pickleball players and influencers share their experiences on platforms like Instagram and TikTok. Follow these accounts for inspiration and to engage with other fans. Commenting on posts or participating in discussions can lead to connections with like-minded individuals.

Utilize Meetup.com: This website is a fantastic resource for finding local pickleball meetups. You can discover events and activities in your area, making it easy to meet fellow players and potential dates in a casual setting.

Connecting Through Dating Apps

Highlight Your Passion: When creating your profile on dating apps like Bumble, Tinder, or Hinge, make sure to mention your love for pickleball. Use specific phrases such as "Pickleball enthusiast" or "Looking for a partner for doubles matches." This will attract other players and serve as an excellent conversation starter.

Use Photos Wisely: Include pictures of yourself playing pickleball or at related events. Action shots can showcase your skills and enthusiasm for the game, making your profile more engaging and relatable.

Be Proactive: Don't wait for matches to come to you. Use the search features on apps to find other players in your area who share your interests. Send friendly messages to initiate conversations and express your interest in playing together.

Engaging in Online Conversations

Start with Pickleball Topics: When you match with someone, kick off the conversation with a pickleball-related question or statement. Ask about their favorite pickleball memory or their go-to strategy on the court. This shared interest can help establish a connection right away.

Share Tips and Experiences: Use your conversations to exchange tips about playing pickleball. Discuss your favorite drills, local courts, or upcoming tournaments. Sharing knowledge can create a bond and showcase your passion for the sport.

Plan a Playdate: Once you've established rapport, suggest meeting up for a game. Whether it's a casual match or a local tournament, playing together can deepen your connection and allow you to see each other in action.

Safety Considerations

Meet in Public Places: Always prioritize safety when arranging to meet someone from a dating app. Choose a public location, such as a local pickleball court or community center, where you can feel comfortable and safe.

Inform a Friend: Let a friend know where you'll be and who you're meeting. Keeping someone informed ensures you have a safety net in place while you enjoy your pickleball date.

Trust Your Instincts: If something feels off during your interactions, don't hesitate to reassess the situation. Your comfort and safety should always come first.

Finding Pickleball Communities While Traveling

Traveling opens up a world of opportunities to engage with new pickleball communities. Whether you're on vacation, attending a conference, or visiting family, finding local pickleball groups or clubs can enhance your trip and allow you to connect with fellow players who share your passion for the game. By utilizing social media, apps, and local events, you can seamlessly integrate pickleball into your travel plans, making new friends and forging lasting connections on and off the court.

Join Pickleball Groups on Facebook:

Look for local pickleball Facebook groups in your destination city. These groups are a great way to connect with players, get tips on where to play, and even find partners for games.

Utilize Meetup:

The **Meetup** app is perfect for finding pickleball gatherings in your area. Search for pickleball events and meetups to join players in your destination.

Follow Local Players on Instagram or Twitter:

Search for local pickleball players or clubs on social media platforms. Following them can provide insight into upcoming events and give you a chance to reach out and connect.

Engage on Reddit:

Visit pickleball subreddits, such as r/Pickleball, to ask about pickleball communities in your travel destination. Reddit users are often eager to share recommendations and connect with fellow enthusiasts.

Download Pickleball Apps:

Explore pickleball-specific apps, such as **Play Your Court** or **TeamUp**, that can help you find games and connect with local players. These platforms often include features for scheduling matches and joining existing games.

Attending Pickleball Tournaments or Events in New Cities

Check Event Calendars:

Research pickleball tournaments and events happening during your travel dates. Websites like **PickleballTournaments.com** list upcoming competitions, allowing you to plan your visit accordingly.

Participate in Local Tournaments:

If you're comfortable, consider signing up for a local tournament. This is a fantastic way to immerse yourself in the community, meet new players, and challenge yourself against different skill levels.

Attend Social Events:

Many clubs host social events or mixers that invite players to meet and play casually. Participating in these gatherings can help you build connections and find potential partners for future games.

Volunteer at Tournaments:

If you're not competing, consider volunteering at a local tournament. It's a great way to get involved, meet players, and enjoy the atmosphere, all while contributing to the success of the event.

Network with Fellow Players:

> While attending tournaments or events, take the time to network with other players. Ask for recommendations on where to play or join them for casual games in the area.

Finding pickleball communities while traveling can enhance your experience and create lasting connections with fellow enthusiasts. By utilizing resources available both online and in your destination, you can seamlessly integrate your love for pickleball into your travel plans. Embrace the opportunity to play in new settings, meet new friends, and enrich your travel adventures through the sport you love. Whether you're competing in tournaments or enjoying casual games, every interaction on the court has the potential to lead to friendships and unforgettable experiences. Happy travels and happy playing!

Chapter 4

Highlighting Pickleball in Your Dating Profile

Pickleball is more than just a fun pastime—it's quickly becoming a favorite sport for people of all ages, especially those in their 50s and beyond. Including pickleball in your dating profile can be a unique and engaging way to connect with potential matches. Here's why highlighting your love for the sport can work in your favor:

A Growing Popularity Across All Ages: Pickleball has experienced a surge in popularity, appealing to players of all skill levels. It combines elements of tennis, badminton, and ping-pong, offering a fun, social, and active experience. Whether you're an experienced player or just starting, mentioning pickleball on your dating profile can be an excellent icebreaker and show that you enjoy staying active.

Perfect for Those 50 and Above: The game has especially gained traction among individuals in their 50s and beyond. It's low-impact yet fast-paced, making it a great option for those who want to stay fit without overexertion. Including it in your profile could signal that you're part of this vibrant, health-conscious community, which could attract others with similar interests.

A Shared Activity for Bonding: Pickleball isn't just about fitness; it's also a great way to connect. Mentioning that you play or want to learn pickleball can open up opportunities for shared experiences and potential first dates. Suggesting a friendly game is not only a casual and low-pressure way to spend time with someone new, but it's also an active, fun, and social way to bond.

Showcasing an Active Lifestyle: Including pickleball in your dating profile sends the message that you're energetic and enjoy an active lifestyle. This can attract those who value health and wellness, and it can spark interest among people looking for a partner who stays physically active.

Adds Personality and Charm: Sharing that you play pickleball also adds a layer of personality to your profile. It shows that you're not only interested in hobbies but that you engage in ones that promote social interaction and community—a desirable trait in any relationship.

Incorporating pickleball into your dating profile is a great way to stand out while promoting both your active lifestyle and fun-loving personality. With its growing popularity, especially among people in their 50s and older, it's likely to catch the attention of potential partners who share similar interests or are looking for an enjoyable way to stay fit. So don't hesitate to showcase your passion for pickleball—you might just serve up a perfect match!

How to Include Pickleball in Your Dating Profile

When it comes to writing your dating profile, mentioning pickleball can be a fantastic way to stand out, showcase your active lifestyle, and attract like-minded individuals. Here are some tips on how to effectively incorporate your love for pickleball into your profile:

Weave It into Your Interests: In the section where you list your hobbies or interests, casually mention pickleball alongside your other favorite activities. For example: *"I'm always up for a fun pickleball game or exploring new outdoor activities on the weekends."*

This keeps it light, approachable, and shows you're active without making it the main focus.

Use It as a Conversation Starter: Including pickleball in your profile can create an easy entry point for someone to strike up a conversation. You could say: *"I recently got hooked on pickleball—anyone else want to join me for a game?"*

This adds an inviting tone and suggests you're open to shared activities.

Highlight Its Social Aspect: Pickleball is known for being a social sport, so you can highlight how you enjoy the camaraderie it brings: *"Love staying active and meeting new people, whether it's on a pickleball court or over coffee."*

This signals that you're approachable, enjoy socializing, and lead a well-rounded life.

Showcase Your Competitive (or Playful) Side: If you're competitive or just love having fun, you can emphasize this in a lighthearted way: *"Warning: I might challenge you to a game of pickleball and won't go easy!"*

It's a fun way to showcase your sense of humor and adds a playful vibe to your profile.

Use It in Your Profile Photos: A picture can say a thousand words! Consider including a candid or action shot of you playing pickleball or holding a paddle. This not only sparks curiosity but also gives potential matches a glimpse of your sporty side and what they can look forward to doing with you.

Invite Pickleball as a Date Idea: Suggesting pickleball as a date can be a fun way to propose something interactive and casual: *"Looking for someone to team up with on the pickleball court—let's see if we're a match on and off the court!"*

It opens the door for playful banter and sets the stage for a fun first date.

Appeal to the 50+ Crowd: If you're aiming to attract someone within the 50+ age group, mentioning pickleball can resonate even more strongly since it's especially popular among this demographic. You could phrase it like: *"Pickleball keeps me fit and is one of my favorite ways to stay active—anyone else in the 50+ club enjoy a good game?"*

This subtly connects with those who are already familiar with or interested in the sport.

By including pickleball in your dating profile in a fun and engaging way, you're not only highlighting an enjoyable hobby but also creating opportunities for connection and conversation with someone who might share your passion or want to learn more. It's a great way to introduce yourself as someone who's active, social, and ready for some lighthearted competition—whether on or off the court!

The Benefits of Mentioning Pickleball in Your Dating Profile

Incorporating pickleball into your dating profile can yield several benefits that extend beyond simply stating your hobbies. Here are some key advantages to highlighting this popular sport:

Aligning Interests with Potential Matches: By showcasing your love for pickleball, you may attract individuals who share the same passion. This alignment of interests can lead to deeper connections and more meaningful interactions.

Breaking the Ice: Pickleball is a fun and approachable sport that serves as an excellent conversation starter. Mentioning it in your profile can help break the ice and encourage potential matches to engage with you. They might ask about your favorite playing spots, your playing style, or even propose a friendly match!

Creating Shared Experiences: Including pickleball in your profile opens the door for shared experiences. You can suggest playing together, attending local tournaments, or participating in pickleball socials, which can lead to memorable dates and strengthen your bond.

Demonstrating a Balanced Lifestyle: Engaging in sports like pickleball indicates a balanced lifestyle. It shows that you prioritize physical activity, social interaction, and fun, which are appealing qualities in a partner. This can make your profile more attractive to those seeking a well-rounded relationship.

Fostering an Active and Engaging Profile: Profiles that mention hobbies or activities tend to be more engaging. By discussing pickleball, you provide insight into your personality, lifestyle, and interests, allowing potential matches to envision shared experiences with you.

Promoting a Health-Conscious Image: Highlighting your involvement in pickleball can portray you as health-conscious and active. This image is especially appealing to individuals looking for a partner who values fitness and well-being, creating a common ground for meaningful discussions.

Building a Sense of Community: Mentioning pickleball can connect you with a community of players, both online and offline. Many people are seeking partners who understand their passions, and showcasing your love for this sport can help you find a compatible match within that community.

Encouraging a Playful Spirit: By discussing pickleball, you demonstrate a playful and adventurous spirit. This quality can be contagious, drawing in potential partners who appreciate a sense of fun and spontaneity in their relationships.

Creating Opportunities for Growth: Including pickleball in your dating profile allows for the potential to grow together as a couple. Whether you're both experienced players or beginners, you can support each other in learning and improving your skills, which fosters collaboration and teamwork.

Showing Openness to New Experiences: Your profile can reflect your openness to new experiences by stating your willingness to learn or play pickleball. This attitude can attract individuals who are similarly adventurous and eager to try new activities together.

In summary, emphasizing your love for pickleball in your dating profile can significantly enhance your chances of connecting with like-minded individuals. The sport's growing popularity, particularly among those in their 50s and beyond, creates ample opportunities for engaging conversations, shared activities, and meaningful connections. So, don't hesitate to let your passion for pickleball shine through in your profile— you might just serve up the perfect match!

Crafting a Catchy Pickleball Tagline

A catchy tagline can enhance your dating profile and make it more memorable. Here are some ideas for pickleball-themed taglines:

"Let's Serve Up Some Fun!"

> This tagline is light-hearted and invites potential matches to engage in playful banter while expressing your enthusiasm for pickleball.

"Looking for My Pickleball Partner in Crime!"

> This fun twist indicates that you're seeking companionship both on and off the court, making it clear that you value relationships as much as the game.

"Life's a Game—Let's Play Pickleball Together!"

This catchy phrase suggests that you approach life with a playful spirit and are looking for someone who shares that mindset.

"Ready to Rally in Life and Love!"

This tagline emphasizes your enthusiasm for pickleball while hinting at your desire for a meaningful relationship.

"Searching for a Double to My Pickleball!"

A clever play on words, this tagline conveys both your passion for the sport and your quest for a romantic connection.

"Pickleball: The Perfect Match for Love!"

This tagline emphasizes the connection between the game and your dating life, making it clear that you're seeking someone who appreciates pickleball as much as you do.

By incorporating your passion for pickleball into your dating profile, you not only attract like-minded individuals but also present a dynamic and engaging image of yourself. Whether it's through sharing your love for the sport or crafting catchy taglines, your dating profile can serve as a reflection of your personality and interests, making it easier for you to connect with potential matches. Feel free to mix and match or modify any of these sentences to better suit your style! Remember, the goal is to showcase your authentic self while having fun and inviting interaction. Happy dating on and off the court!

100 Taglines to Showcase Your Pickleball Passion

1. I love playing pickleball on weekends—join me!

2. Looking for someone to challenge me on the pickleball court.

3. I'm passionate about staying active and pickleball is my favorite sport.

4. Pickleball has become my new obsession; want to join?

5. Let's meet up for a game of pickleball!

6. I enjoy the social aspect of pickleball; it's a blast!

7. Pickleball is my go-to for staying fit and having fun.

8. Who's up for a friendly pickleball match?

9. I'd love to find a partner who enjoys pickleball as much as I do.

10. Pickleball: the perfect blend of competition and fun.

11. I'm all about good vibes and pickleball games.

12. My favorite way to unwind is playing pickleball.

13. I recently discovered pickleball—it's a game-changer!

14. I can't resist a spontaneous pickleball game!

15. Let's grab some paddles and hit the pickleball court!

16. Pickleball is my favorite way to socialize and stay fit.

17. If you love pickleball, we'll get along just fine!

18. Let's spice things up with a game of pickleball!

19. I'm looking for someone to be my pickleball partner.

20. Pickleball keeps me active and happy.

21. I'm excited to meet fellow pickleball enthusiasts!

22. Want to learn how to play pickleball together?

23. I love the community around pickleball.

24. Pickleball is my favorite way to meet new people.

25. I'm always up for a good match of pickleball.

26. I appreciate anyone who can handle a pickleball challenge!

27. Nothing beats a sunny day of pickleball with friends.

28. I like to keep my weekends busy with pickleball matches.

29. Looking to share some laughs and pickleball games.

30. Pickleball is a great way to keep fit and have fun.

31. I'm passionate about improving my pickleball skills!

32. Let's bond over some pickleball action!

33. I can't wait to share my love for pickleball with someone special.

34. Pickleball is my favorite sport—how about you?

35. Want to team up for a pickleball tournament?

36. I love the thrill of pickleball matches.

37. My weekends revolve around pickleball and good company.

38. I'm all about the fun and fitness of pickleball.

39. Looking for someone who shares my love for pickleball.

40. I enjoy mixing exercise with socializing through pickleball.

41. Pickleball is the best way to stay active and meet new friends.

42. Want to learn some pickleball strategies together?

43. I'm always game for a friendly round of pickleball!

44. Pickleball: my happy place.

45. If you love pickleball, we'll have so much in common.

46. I've met some amazing people through pickleball.

47. Playing pickleball brings me so much joy!

48. Let's see if we can ace our pickleball game!

49. I'm on a mission to find the best pickleball courts around.

50. I'm all about fun competition on the pickleball court.

51. Pickleball is the sport that makes my heart race!

52. I love how pickleball brings people together.

53. Want to hit the court for some pickleball fun?

54. My ideal date involves playing pickleball.

55. I'm excited to find someone who loves pickleball, too!

56. Pickleball is the perfect mix of strategy and fun.

57. I can't get enough of pickleball!

58. I love the energy of a good pickleball match.

59. Let's bring some fun to the court with pickleball!

60. I thrive on the camaraderie of pickleball games.

61. Pickleball is my favorite way to stay active.

62. Who's ready for a pickleball adventure?

63. Pickleball is my happy hour!

64. I enjoy playing pickleball for the exercise and the fun.

65. If you're a pickleball player, let's connect!

66. Pickleball brings out my competitive side!

67. I'm looking for someone who can match my pickleball energy.

68. I love the strategy involved in pickleball matches.

69. Nothing beats a great game of pickleball with friends.

70. Pickleball is the highlight of my week!

71. Let's have some fun on the pickleball court!

72. Pickleball is more than a sport; it's a lifestyle for me.

73. I enjoy the challenge of improving my pickleball skills.

74. I can't wait to play pickleball with you!

75. Let's bring our best pickleball game to the court!

76. I love meeting new people while playing pickleball.

77. Pickleball is my favorite way to unwind after a long week.

78. I'm ready to make some pickleball memories!

79. Want to join me for a fun pickleball session?

80. I'm all about the laughter and fun of pickleball.

81. Pickleball is my weekend warrior activity!

82. I love how pickleball keeps me active and social.

83. I'm looking for someone to enjoy pickleball with.

84. Want to swap pickleball tips?

85. I enjoy the friendly competition of pickleball matches.

86. Pickleball is a fantastic way to meet new friends.

87. I'm passionate about promoting pickleball in my community.

88. My favorite court is where the pickleball action happens!

89. I can't wait to share my love for pickleball on our first date!

90. Let's create some pickleball stories together!

91. I enjoy the thrill of a close pickleball match.

92. Pickleball is the sport that makes me smile!

93. Who's in for a fun pickleball tournament?

94. I thrive in the exciting atmosphere of pickleball.

95. I love how pickleball combines fitness and fun.

96. Let's find some time to play pickleball together!

97. I'm all about sharing the joy of pickleball.

98. Pickleball keeps my spirits high!

99. I enjoy every moment spent on the pickleball court.

100. Pickleball is my favorite way to stay active and make connections!

Chapter 5

Empowering Women in the Pickleball Dating Scene

As more women embrace pickleball, the sport offers unique opportunities for connection and romance. Whether you're new to the game or a seasoned player, this chapter will provide valuable advice tailored specifically for women navigating the pickleball dating scene. From building confidence on the court to effectively communicating your intentions, this chapter aims to empower women to thrive in their pickleball relationships.

Embrace Your Strengths

Build Confidence

Confidence is Key: Recognize the skills and strengths you bring to the game. Celebrate your achievements, whether it's mastering a tricky shot or successfully playing in a tournament. Confidence on the court translates to confidence in your dating life.

Know Your Value: Understand that your passion for pickleball and your commitment to improving make you an attractive partner. Approach dating with the mindset that you have much to offer in a relationship.

Be Open and Approachable

Body Language Matters: Keep your posture open and inviting. Smile and make eye contact with other players. This non-verbal communication can make you appear more approachable and friendly.

Engage in Conversations: Don't hesitate to strike up conversations with fellow players. Ask about their favorite shots or recent games. Showing genuine interest in others can help you build connections naturally.

Set Clear Intentions

Be Honest About Your Goals: Before diving into the dating scene, take some time to reflect on what you're looking for—whether it's casual dating, friendship, or a serious relationship. Being clear about your intentions can help you navigate your interactions with potential partners more effectively.

Communicate Openly: When you meet someone you're interested in, communicate your feelings and intentions. Open dialogue can build trust and prevent misunderstandings in the early stages of dating.

Create Inclusive Environments

Sense of belonging

Foster a Welcoming Atmosphere: As a woman in pickleball, you have the power to create a sense of belonging for other players. By being friendly and inclusive, you can help establish a positive community that attracts potential partners.

Organize Social Events: Consider hosting social events or mixers for your local pickleball community. This not only helps you meet new people but also allows you to showcase your leadership and organizational skills.

Navigate Challenges with Grace

Addressing Stereotypes: Unfortunately, women in sports can sometimes face stereotypes or biases. Approach these challenges with confidence and resilience. Stay true to your passion for pickleball and don't let negativity deter you from enjoying the game or exploring dating opportunities.

Balancing Competition and Connection: While it's great to be competitive, remember that the primary goal of dating is connection. Keep the spirit of fun alive in your games and interactions and prioritize building relationships over winning every match.

Prioritize Self-Care and Wellness

Take Care of Yourself: Prioritizing your physical and mental health can boost your confidence and make you more attractive to potential partners. Incorporate regular exercise, healthy eating, and self-care routines into your life.

Reflect on Your Experiences: After dates or interactions with potential partners, take time to reflect on your feelings and experiences. Understanding what resonates with you can help you make informed decisions about future relationships.

Stay True to Yourself

Be Authentic: Embrace your unique qualities and interests. Authenticity is attractive, and being yourself will help attract the right kind of partner who appreciates you for who you are.

Don't Compromise Your Values: In your quest for love, remember to stay true to your values and beliefs. Look for someone who shares your passion for pickleball and respects your boundaries.

As a woman in the pickleball dating scene, you have the power to shape your experiences and create meaningful connections. By embracing your strengths, communicating openly, and fostering inclusivity, you'll not only enhance your dating journey but also contribute positively to the pickleball community. Remember, dating is about enjoying the journey, learning about yourself, and discovering the joy of connecting with others through the game you love. With confidence and authenticity, you can thrive both on the court and in your romantic pursuits.

Chapter 6

A Man's Guide to Navigating the Pickleball Dating Scene

For men looking to explore romantic connections within the world of pickleball, the court offers a unique environment to meet potential partners who share a passion for the game. This chapter will provide actionable advice for men to help them approach dating in the pickleball community with confidence, respect, and authenticity. From honing your skills on the court to understanding the dynamics of dating, this chapter is designed to empower men to make meaningful connections.

Create a Supportive Community

Be a Supportive Player

Encourage Others: Foster a positive environment on the court by cheering for your fellow players and offering words of encouragement. This not only helps create a supportive community but also makes you more appealing to potential partners who value teamwork and camaraderie.

Share Your Knowledge: If you have experience or expertise in pickleball, consider sharing tips and strategies with less experienced players. This can build rapport and showcase your willingness to help others grow in the sport.

Approach with Confidence

Confidence Over Cockiness: Confidence is attractive, but there's a fine line between confidence and arrogance. Carry yourself with assurance but remain humble and approachable. Show interest in others rather than dominating conversations.

Be Mindful of Body Language: Your body language speaks volumes. Maintain an open and relaxed posture, make eye contact, and smile. These non-verbal cues can make you appear more approachable and inviting.

Communicate Clearly

Be Honest About Your Intentions: When you meet someone you're interested in, communicate your feelings clearly and respectfully. Being upfront about your intentions can prevent misunderstandings and set a solid foundation for any potential relationship.

Listen Actively: Engage in active listening when talking to potential partners. Show genuine interest in their stories and experiences and respond thoughtfully. This can help you build a deeper connection based on mutual respect.

Build Relationships Beyond the Court

Mix, Mingle and Play

Organize Social Activities: Consider hosting or organizing social events related to pickleball, such as mixers or friendly tournaments. These gatherings can help break the ice and create opportunities for meaningful interactions outside of regular games.

Connect Through Shared Interests: While pickleball is a great common ground, try to discover additional shared interests with potential partners. This could lead to exciting date ideas and deeper conversations.

Be Respectful and Considerate

Respect Boundaries: Always be mindful of personal space and boundaries, especially when getting to know someone. Pay attention to verbal and non-verbal cues that indicate comfort or discomfort.

Handle Rejection Gracefully: If someone isn't interested, respect their feelings and don't take it personally. Handling rejection with grace reflects maturity and can leave the door open for friendship or future interactions.

Dress for Success

Choose Appropriate Attire: Dressing well for pickleball is important, not just for performance but also for making a good impression. Wear comfortable athletic wear that fits well and reflects your style, while also being practical for the game.

Personal Grooming: Take the time to present yourself well. A well-groomed appearance can boost your confidence and create a positive impression on potential partners.

Focus on Personal Growth

Improve Your Game: Dedicate time to improving your pickleball skills. This not only enhances your performance but also shows your commitment to personal growth, which can be attractive to potential partners.

Develop Your Interests: While pickleball may be a shared interest, nurturing your hobbies and passions outside the sport will make you a more well-rounded individual. This can enrich your conversations and make you more interesting to others.

Be Patient and Authentic

Take Your Time: Building connections takes time. Don't rush the dating process. Allow relationships to develop naturally and enjoy the journey of getting to know others.

Stay True to Yourself: Authenticity is essential in forming meaningful connections. Be yourself and allow your personality to shine. This will help you attract someone who appreciates you for who you truly are.

Dating within the pickleball community offers men a unique opportunity to meet and connect with potential partners who share their passion for the game. By approaching the dating scene with confidence, respect, and authenticity, you can foster meaningful relationships that extend beyond the court. Embrace the experience, enjoy the camaraderie, and remember that every match is not just about the game—it's also about the potential for love and connection in your life. With the right mindset and approach, you can successfully navigate the pickleball dating scene and find a partner who shares your passion for both the sport and life.

Chapter 7

Getting Started: Preparing for Pickleball Dating

Assessing Your Goals: Fun vs. Serious Relationships

Before diving into the world of pickleball dating, it's crucial to assess your relationship goals. Understanding what you're looking for will guide your approach and help you connect with like-minded individuals on the court. Whether you seek fun, casual interactions or meaningful, long-term relationships, being clear about your intentions will help shape your experience and increase your chances of finding the right match.

Fun and Casual

If your primary aim is to enjoy the game and meet new people without the pressure of a serious commitment, embracing a fun and casual dating mindset is key. This approach allows you to focus on enjoying the sport, building friendships, and exploring potential connections without rushing into a relationship. Here are some strategies to maximize your enjoyment while keeping things light:

Participate in Group Activities: Look for group pickleball events, leagues, or social tournaments. These settings foster a relaxed atmosphere where players can engage without the pressure of one-on-one interactions. Enjoying the game together can create a sense of camaraderie that naturally lends itself to friendships— and possibly more.

Embrace Spontaneity: Be open to spontaneous outings and casual encounters. After a fun game, suggest grabbing a bite to eat with fellow players or heading to a local café to unwind. This relaxed approach allows connections to develop organically, giving you the chance to meet others while keeping expectations low.

Build Friendships First: Focus on building friendships with fellow players. Many successful relationships start as friendships, so investing time in getting to know others can pay off later. Share your experiences on the court, celebrate each other's victories, and support one another through losses.

Maintain an Open Mind: While your initial intent might be to keep things casual, remain open to the possibility of deeper connections. You may find that a friendship evolves into something more significant without the pressure of forced romantic expectations.

Enjoy the Journey: Remember that dating, like pickleball, is meant to be enjoyable. Relish the opportunity to meet diverse individuals and experience new perspectives. By keeping a lighthearted attitude, you'll create a more enjoyable environment for yourself and others.

Serious Intentions

If you're looking for a meaningful, long-term relationship, it's essential to communicate your intentions clearly to potential partners. This doesn't mean you can't have fun while dating; instead, being upfront about your desire for something serious can help filter out individuals who may not share the same goals. Here are some strategies to cultivate deeper connections:

Communicate Your Intentions: When you meet someone you're interested in, don't hesitate to express your intentions. You can do this naturally by discussing your relationship goals during casual conversations on the court. Open dialogue sets a solid foundation and helps ensure you're both on the same page.

Engage in One-on-One Matches: While group play is fun, consider scheduling one-on-one matches with individuals you find intriguing. These matches provide a more intimate setting to learn about one another's personalities, interests, and backgrounds. Use this time to build rapport and assess compatibility.

Participate in Singles Events: Look for events specifically designed for singles in the pickleball community. These gatherings often feature structured activities that encourage interaction among participants. Engaging in singles events can help you connect with others who share similar relationship goals and are eager to meet someone special.

Foster Deeper Connections: Pay attention to individuals with whom you share a strong connection. Explore common interests beyond pickleball, such as hobbies, travel, or family values. By nurturing these connections, you'll be better equipped to transition from casual interactions to a more meaningful relationship.

Be Patient: Finding a serious relationship often takes time and patience. While it's important to communicate your intentions, allow relationships to develop naturally. Enjoy the process of getting to know someone without putting pressure on the situation.

Hybrid Approach

Many players find themselves in between these two extremes, desiring to enjoy the social aspects of pickleball while remaining open to the possibility of a serious relationship. This hybrid approach offers flexibility and can lead to fulfilling experiences. Here are some strategies for navigating this balance:

Stay Adaptable: Embrace the idea that your relationship goals may evolve over time. You might start with a focus on fun and friendships, only to discover that a deeper connection has formed with someone you initially considered a casual acquaintance. Staying open to this possibility allows you to explore meaningful relationships while enjoying the sport.

Build a Diverse Social Circle: Surround yourself with a mix of players who share both casual and serious intentions. This diverse social circle allows you to enjoy the social aspects of pickleball while remaining open to the potential for deeper connections.

Engage in Varied Activities: Participate in both casual group events and structured singles activities. This strategy enables you to meet various individuals and fosters an environment where friendships can flourish alongside potential romantic interests. By exposing yourself to different social settings, you increase your chances of finding someone who aligns with your goals.

Communicate Regularly: Keep lines of communication open with your pickleball partners. As relationships evolve, regularly check in with yourself and others about intentions. This open dialogue helps manage expectations and ensures that everyone remains on the same page.

Enjoy the Journey: Whether you ultimately seek casual connections or a serious relationship, remember to enjoy the journey. Allowing relationships to develop organically can lead to unexpected joys, friendships, and possibly even lasting love.

As you prepare to embark on your pickleball dating journey, assessing your goals is crucial for fostering connections that align with your intentions. Whether you're seeking fun and casual encounters, a serious relationship, or a blend of both, understanding what you want will guide your approach on and off the court. By maintaining an open mind and embracing the spirit of the game, you can navigate the world of pickleball dating with confidence, creating meaningful connections that enhance your life and enrich your experiences.

Chapter 8

Dressing for Success: What to Wear on the Court

Your attire can play a significant role in how you feel and how others perceive you on the court. Dressing appropriately for pickleball can enhance your performance and make you feel confident while socializing. Here's a comprehensive guide to help you make the right fashion choices for a successful day on the court.

Comfortable Athletic Wear

Moisture-Wicking Fabrics: When selecting your clothing, prioritize moisture-wicking materials that pull sweat away from your skin. Fabrics such as polyester or nylon not only keep you cool but also prevent chafing during play. This comfort can boost your confidence, allowing you to focus on the game and your interactions with fellow players.

Choose the Right Fit: Pick attire that allows for ease of movement. Comfortable shorts, skirts, or athletic leggings should fit well without being too tight or too loose. You want to ensure your clothing won't restrict your movements during intense matches, allowing you to move swiftly and with agility.

Breathable Tops: Opt for breathable tops that encourage airflow. Look for short-sleeved or tank-style shirts that allow for maximum ventilation. This will help regulate your body temperature during those fast-paced games.

Supportive Sports Bras: For women, a supportive sports bra is crucial. Choose one that provides enough support for dynamic movements without sacrificing comfort. This will allow you to stay focused on your game rather than adjusting your clothing.

Footwear Matters

Proper Footwear: The right shoes are essential for injury prevention and improved performance on the court. Pickleball requires quick lateral movements, so consider investing in shoes specifically designed for court sports. Look for features such as reinforced toe boxes, cushioning, and non-marking soles that provide traction.

Lightweight and Agile: Your footwear should be lightweight, allowing you to move with agility. This can significantly enhance your performance and make you feel more confident during play. Additionally, well-fitted shoes can help prevent blisters and discomfort, letting you concentrate on your game.

Personalized Style: While function is essential, you can also express your personal style through your choice of footwear. Opt for colors or patterns that reflect your personality, making you feel even more connected to your attire.

Accessorize Thoughtfully

Fun Accessories: Accessories can add flair to your outfit while serving practical purposes. Consider wearing colorful visors, headbands, or wristbands that reflect your personality. These items not only keep sweat at bay but can also serve as conversation starters.

Functional Gear: Choose accessories that enhance your performance. For instance, moisture-wicking headbands can keep hair out of your face and absorb sweat, allowing you to maintain focus during games. Look for items that marry style and functionality.

Hydration and Snacks: Don't forget to accessorize with a stylish water bottle or a small bag for healthy snacks. Staying hydrated and energized is crucial for maintaining your performance level, and having these essentials can keep you prepared for socializing on and off the court.

Stay Safe from the Elements

Sun Protection: Depending on the weather, sun protection is vital. Sunscreen is a must, especially for outdoor play. Apply a broad-spectrum sunscreen with a high SPF before heading to the court to protect your skin from harmful UV rays.

Sunglasses and Hats: Sunglasses with UV protection can shield your eyes from glare while enhancing your visibility on the court. Pair them with a lightweight, breathable hat or visor to keep the sun out of your face. Look for styles that complement your athletic look while providing necessary coverage.

Layer for Comfort: In cooler weather, layers are your best friend. A light jacket or zip-up hoodie can keep you comfortable during warm-up and cool down. Opt for materials that are breathable yet provide warmth, so you don't overheat when you start playing.

Personal Hygiene and Grooming

Good Hygiene Matters: Good hygiene and grooming go a long way in making a positive impression. Shower before heading to the court, and ensure your hair is clean and styled.

Neat Hair for Comfort: Keeping your hair neat while playing is important for comfort and confidence. If you have long hair, consider using caps or visors designed with openings for ponytails or buns. This keeps your hair in place during intense play and ensures a polished look.

Absorb Sweat with Headbands: Breathable headbands are an excellent choice for absorbing sweat and keeping hair away from your face. They add a sporty touch to your look while maintaining practicality.

Light Fragrance: A light spritz of fragrance can help you feel fresh and confident as you engage with others on the court. Just be mindful not to overdo it; a subtle scent is best for sports settings.

Confidence Through Appearance: Remember, confidence often stems from feeling good about yourself. Taking the time to present your best self on the court can elevate your mood and enhance your interactions with fellow players.

Embrace the Game with Style

By preparing thoughtfully for your pickleball journey—assessing your relationship goals, finding local leagues, and dressing for success—you'll be well-equipped to embrace the excitement of meeting new people and forging meaningful connections through this engaging sport. Dress comfortably, accessorize creatively, and enjoy the game; let love find you on the court!

Chapter 9

The Pickleball Dating Funnel

Creating Your Ideal Partner Profile

The first step in the pickleball dating funnel is to create a clear and compelling profile of your ideal partner. This profile will help you attract individuals who align with your values and relationship goals. Here's how to get started:

Define Key Qualities: Start by listing the essential qualities you seek in a partner. Consider factors such as personality traits, interests, lifestyle, and relationship goals. For instance, you might prioritize traits like kindness, a sense of humor, or a passion for fitness.

Assess Shared Interests: Since you're both participating in pickleball, think about how this shared interest can translate into other aspects of life. Do you value active living, outdoor adventures, or a love for community events? Highlight these interests in your profile to attract like-minded individuals.

Be Realistic: While it's important to have standards, also be open to possibilities. Your ideal partner might not check every box but could still be a great match for you. Emphasize flexibility in your profile to allow for connections that may surprise you.

Visualize the Future: Consider what a relationship with your ideal partner might look like. Do you envision playing pickleball together, traveling, or enjoying game nights? Having a clear picture of your desired relationship dynamics can help you articulate your needs effectively.

Attracting the Right Players: Your Personal Marketing Strategy

Now that you have a profile of your ideal partner, it's time to implement a personal marketing strategy to attract the right individuals to your pickleball dating journey:

Engage on the Court: Use your time on the court as an opportunity to showcase your personality. Smile, be friendly, and engage in conversations with fellow players. Your enthusiasm for the game will attract those who share your passion.

Participate Actively: Attend various pickleball events, leagues, and social gatherings. The more active you are within the community, the higher your chances of meeting potential partners. Use these opportunities to demonstrate your commitment to the sport and your desire to connect.

Utilize Social Media: Leverage social media platforms to showcase your pickleball adventures. Share photos, stories, and experiences from your games. Engaging content can attract the attention of potential partners and create a sense of familiarity before you even meet.

Network with Friends: Don't hesitate to let your friends know that you're interested in meeting someone special through pickleball. They may know someone who fits your ideal partner profile and can introduce you in a relaxed setting.

Create a Memorable Presence: Whether it's through your style, your positive attitude, or your commitment to the game, ensure you stand out. Being memorable increases the likelihood that potential partners will remember you and want to connect.

Strategies for Filtering Potential Partners

Once you start meeting potential partners, it's essential to have strategies in place for filtering candidates to ensure compatibility. Here are some effective techniques:

Initial Conversations: Engage in open and honest discussions about your interests, values, and relationship goals. Pay attention to how potential partners respond to your questions—this can reveal a lot about their intentions and compatibility.

Play Together: Organizing casual matches or participating in mixed doubles can provide insights into a potential partner's playing style and sportsmanship. Observing how they interact with others on the court can help gauge their character.

Group Activities: Consider inviting potential partners to group events or clinics. This setting allows you to observe how they engage with others while still having fun. Group dynamics can provide a clearer picture of their personality and values.

Set Boundaries: It's important to establish and communicate your boundaries early in the process. Whether it's regarding the pace of dating or specific relationship goals, being upfront will help filter out those who do not align with your needs.

Trust Your Instincts: Finally, listen to your intuition. If something feels off, don't hesitate to reassess your connection with a potential partner. Trusting your instincts can help you avoid red flags and focus on individuals who genuinely resonate with you.

By implementing these strategies within the pickleball dating funnel—creating your ideal partner profile, attracting the right players, and filtering potential partners—you can navigate the dating scene with confidence and purpose. Enjoy the process and let the connections you build lead to meaningful relationships on and off the court!

Chapter 10

The Art of Flirting on the Court

Body Language and Signals in Pickleball

Flirting on the pickleball court requires a keen understanding of body language and non-verbal cues. Here are some essential elements to consider:

Open Posture: Maintain an open and inviting stance while playing. Facing your potential partner directly, with your arms relaxed and uncrossed, signals that you are approachable and interested in engaging with them.

Eye Contact: Eye contact is a powerful tool for connection. Locking eyes with someone while playing or during a break can create intimacy and demonstrate interest. A friendly smile can also enhance this connection and make the interaction more inviting.

Playful Gestures: Use playful gestures, such as a light tap on the shoulder after a good point or a playful mimicry of their playing style, to create a fun atmosphere. These gestures can serve as icebreakers and signal your interest in a lighthearted manner.

Mirroring: Subtly mirroring the body language of a fellow player can create a sense of rapport and connection. If they lean in, try leaning in too; if they smile, reciprocate with a smile. This non-verbal communication helps establish a bond.

Positive Energy: Radiate positivity while on the court. Laugh, celebrate good shots, and show enthusiasm. Your energy can be contagious, attracting like-minded individuals who appreciate your vibrant spirit.

How to Start Conversations with Fellow Players

Starting conversations on the court can be simple and enjoyable with the right approach. Here are some strategies to initiate engaging dialogues:

Comment on the Game: Begin by commenting on the match or a specific play. Phrases like, "That was an impressive shot!" or "I loved that rally—let's keep that energy going!" can lead to more in-depth discussions about techniques and strategies.

Ask for Tips: Don't hesitate to ask fellow players for advice or tips on improving your game. This not only opens the door for conversation but also shows that you value their expertise, creating a sense of camaraderie.

Introduce Yourself: If you see someone you'd like to get to know better, introduce yourself with a smile and a friendly tone. Sharing your name and a little about your pickleball journey can set the stage for deeper conversations.

Use Humor: Light-hearted jokes or playful banter about the game can break the ice and create a relaxed atmosphere. A good laugh can quickly dissolve any awkwardness and pave the way for a more genuine connection.

Invite Group Play: If the chemistry feels right, invite them to join you for a group game or a friendly practice session. Group activities foster interaction and allow you to get to know one another in a fun, low-pressure setting.

100 pickleball jokes to keep the laughter rolling on and off the court:

1. Why did the pickleball player bring a ladder to the game?
   Because they wanted to reach new heights!

2. What do you call a pickleball player who never loses?
   A dill-igent competitor!

3. Why did the pickleball player get kicked off the team?
   Because they kept serving up bad puns!

4. How do pickleball players stay cool during a match?
   They always keep their composure!

5. What did the pickle say to the ball?
   "You're the zest!"

6. Why was the pickleball court always so clean?
   Because it had great court-ship!

7. What do you call a pickleball tournament for comedians?
The Laugh-a-ball Classic!

8. Why do pickleball players make terrible secret agents?
Because they always serve up their locations!

9. What's a pickleball player's favorite music genre?
Rock and roll—the best way to serve it up!

10. Why did the pickleball player bring string to the game?
To tie the score!

11. How does a pickleball player apologize?
They say, "I'm sorry, I didn't mean to fault!"

12. Why do pickleball players love socializing?
Because they can't resist a good rally!

13. What did the judge say to the pickleball player?
"You've got a great serve, but that was a fault!"

14. Why was the pickleball game so easy to understand?
Because it had clear rules—no pickle-ing around!

15. What did the pickleball say when it won a match?
"I'm feeling dill-lighted!"

16. Why did the cucumber join the pickleball team?
To become a pickle champion!

17. What's a pickleball player's favorite exercise?
Serving up some cardio!

18. Why did the pickleball player always bring a pencil?
In case they needed to draw a line!

19. How do pickleball players greet each other?
"Let's paddle on!"

20. Why did the pickleball player break up with their partner?
They just couldn't find the right match!

21. What did the pickleball say to the net?
"You're really catching my attention!"

22. Why are pickleball players so good at math?
Because they know how to calculate their angles!

23. How do you know a pickleball player is a good friend?
They always have your back (court)!

24. What do you call a pickleball enthusiast?
A dill-lightful person!

25. Why did the pickleball player bring a suitcase?
Because they were going on a paddle trip!

26. What's a pickleball player's favorite animal?
A serve-alot!

27. Why do pickleball players never get lost?
They always follow the court lines!

28. How did the pickleball player feel after winning?
On top of the world (or the net)!

29. What do you call a pickleball match in space?
A cosmic rally!

30. Why did the tomato refuse to play pickleball?
Because it couldn't handle the pressure!

31. What did the pickleball player say to their doubles partner?
"Let's make a great team—together we're un-pickle-able!"

32. Why are pickleball courts great for parties?
Because they always have great energy!

33. What do you call a pickleball player who loves to dance?
A real swing-er!

34. Why did the pickleball player start a band?
Because they had great rhythm!

35. What's a pickleball player's favorite snack?
Dill pickle chips!

36. Why do pickleball players make great storytellers?
They always serve up great tales!

37. What do you call a pickleball champion?
A court hero!

38. Why was the pickleball player so confident?
Because they had a solid game plan!

39. How do you know a pickleball player is friendly?
They're always ready for a warm-up!

40. What do you call a pickleball game in the rain?
A slippery serve!

41. Why did the pickleball player refuse to share their secrets?
Because they were afraid of giving away their serve!

42. What did one pickleball paddle say to the other?
"Let's stick together!"

43. How do pickleball players keep their cool?
They always stay in the zone!

44. What's a pickleball player's favorite game?
One that's served fresh!

45. Why did the pickleball player break up with their partner?
They had too many faults in their relationship!

46. What did the pickleball player say after a good rally?
"That was some serious court magic!"

47. How do you cheer up a sad pickleball player?
Tell them they've got great potential!

48. What's a pickleball player's favorite movie?
"The Pickleball Diaries!"

49. Why did the pickleball player never get bored?
Because they always had a new match to play!

50. What do you call a pickleball player who can't stop talking?
A real chatter-paddle!

51. Why did the pickleball player refuse to play at night?
Because they didn't want to deal with shadowy opponents!

52. What's a pickleball player's motto?
"Serve it up with style!"

53. How do you spot a pickleball enthusiast?
They're always looking for a game!

54. Why did the pickleball player visit the therapist?
To work on their emotional rallies!

55. What do you call a pickleball party?
A pickle-palooza!

56. Why was the pickleball player always invited to gatherings?
Because they were a great court-side companion!

57. What's a pickleball player's favorite drink?
Pickle juice lemonade!

58. Why did the pickleball player love summer?
Because it meant outdoor matches!

59. What do you call a pickleball champion who loves to travel?
A global player!

60. Why do pickleball players make good comedians?
They always know how to deliver a punchline!

61. How does a pickleball player celebrate a win?
With a big dill party!

62. What did the pickleball player say when they won a trophy?
"This is a real game-changer!"

63. Why did the cucumber start playing pickleball?
To become a pickleball legend!

64. What's a pickleball player's favorite type of humor?
Punny jokes!

65. Why did the pickleball match get canceled?
Because of a sour mood!

66. What do you call a pickleball paddle that tells jokes?
A funny-racket!

67. How do you throw a pickleball-themed party?
With plenty of serving and smashing fun!

68. Why did the pickleball player always carry a map?
To find the best courts in town!

69. What do you call a pickleball tournament for animals?
The Furry Racket!

70. Why did the pickleball player start a cooking show?
To share their favorite pickle recipes!

71. What's a pickleball player's favorite time of year?
The pickleball season!

72. Why did the pickleball player apply for a job?
To score some extra dough!

73. How do you compliment a pickleball player?
"You've got some serious skills on the court!"

74. Why was the pickleball player great at solving problems?
Because they always knew how to serve up solutions!

75. What do you call a pickleball player who loves the beach?
A sandy server!

76. Why did the pickleball player always wear sunglasses?
To look cool on the court!

77. What's a pickleball player's favorite childhood game?
Hopscotch—because they love to jump around!

78. Why did the pickleball player join a band?
To play the "paddle" guitar!

79. How do pickleball players stay fit?
By serving up their daily exercise!

80. What do you call a pickleball player who loves adventure?
A thrill-seeker on the court!

81. Why do pickleball players love to socialize?
Because they enjoy making new friends while playing!

82. What's a pickleball player's favorite workout?
Cardio with a side of fun!

83. Why did the pickleball player refuse to play cards?
Because they didn't want to deal with any more faults!

84. What do you call a pickleball game with only friends?

A friendly match!

85. Why did the pickleball player always carry a notebook?
To keep track of their "serve"-ious notes!

86. What do you call a pickleball player who loves to dance?
A "paddle" dancer!

87. How do pickleball players like their sandwiches?
With a big pickle on the side!

88. Why was the pickleball player always calm?
Because they knew how to stay in the "zone!"

89. What do you call a pickleball player who tells tall tales?
A "serve-teller!"

90. Why did the pickleball player love gardening?
Because they enjoyed watching things grow!

91. What did the pickleball coach say during practice?
"Time to serve up some hard work!"

92. Why did the pickleball player become a teacher?
To serve knowledge to their students!

93. What's a pickleball player's favorite vacation?
Anywhere with great courts and sunshine!

94. Why did the pickleball player bring a blanket?
To keep warm during those chilly night matches!

95. What do you call a pickleball player with a sweet tooth?
A candy server!

96. Why did the pickleball player start a blog?
To serve up their experiences and tips!

97. What's a pickleball player's favorite type of movie?
Anything with a great plot twist!

98. Why did the pickleball player get a haircut?
To look fresh on the court!

99. What do you call a pickleball match that ends in laughter?
A "serve"-ious good time!

100. Why did the pickleball player bring string to the match?
To tie up the score!

I hope these jokes bring a smile to your face and are perfect for sharing with your fellow pickleball enthusiasts!

Tips for Complimenting Skills and Building Rapport

Compliments can go a long way in building rapport with fellow players and creating a positive environment. Here are some tips for delivering effective compliments:

Be Specific: Instead of generic compliments, focus on specific skills or plays that impressed you. For example, "Your backhand is incredible! I can't believe how consistently you nail those shots!" This shows genuine appreciation and attention to their abilities.

Encourage and Support: If you notice someone struggling or trying a new technique, offer supportive words. Phrases like, "You're improving every game—keep it up!" can boost their confidence and demonstrate your interest.

Celebrate Achievements: When a fellow player wins a match or achieves a personal best, make sure to celebrate their success. Saying something like, "Congratulations on that win! You played fantastically!" fosters a sense of connection and goodwill.

Follow Up: After complimenting someone, continue the conversation by asking about their pickleball journey or future goals. This shows you're interested in them as a person, not just as a player, and can deepen your rapport.

Be Genuine: Authenticity is key. Ensure that your compliments are sincere and reflect your true feelings. People can sense insincerity, so focus on what you genuinely appreciate about their skills or sportsmanship.

By mastering the art of flirting on the pickleball court—understanding body language, initiating conversations, and complimenting skills— you'll enhance your social interactions and increase your chances of building meaningful connections. Embrace the fun, engage with others, and let the court be a backdrop for both competition and romance! These messages will make your crush feel appreciated and recognized for their efforts!

100 Ways to Celebrate Pickleball Success and Compliment Your Crush

1. "Wow, that was an incredible match—you were on fire!"
2. "Congrats on the win! You totally owned the court today."
3. "Your game was unstoppable! So impressive!"
4. "That victory was all yours—well-deserved!"
5. "You make winning look so easy—amazing job!"
6. "You were absolutely amazing out there!"
7. "That was such a powerful performance—congratulations!"
8. "You crushed it! What an awesome game!"
9. "Your skills are next-level—congratulations on that win!"
10. "You made every shot count—so proud of you!"
11. "Congrats! You played like a pro today!"
12. "Your precision on the court was incredible—well done!"
13. "Every serve was perfect—you're a pickleball superstar!"
14. "That game was flawless—so happy for your success!"
15. "You were on point with every shot—congratulations!"
16. "What an incredible performance! You totally earned that win."
17. "You're amazing—your pickleball skills just keep getting better!"
18. "Your focus and dedication paid off big time!"
19. "You played with such confidence—congratulations!"
20. "You're a natural—such a brilliant game today!"
21. "Congrats on the win! You handled every challenge like a pro."
22. "Your energy and enthusiasm on the court are unbeatable!"
23. "You totally nailed it—so proud of your effort and win!"

24. "That was some killer strategy—congrats on your well-earned victory!"

25. "Every move you made was spot-on—what a game!"

26. "You played with such skill and grace—congratulations!"

27. "I'm still in awe of how awesome you were today—well done!"

28. "You were an absolute star out there—so proud of you!"

29. "That match was all you—you gave it your all!"

30. "You played smart and strong—congratulations on an epic win!"

31. "Your game was pure perfection—so happy for you!"

32. "You handled every play with such ease—amazing job!"

33. "Congrats! You made winning look effortless today."

34. "I knew you'd be unstoppable on the court—fantastic game!"

35. "You were unbeatable today—so proud of you!"

36. "Your talent shines every time you play—congrats on another win!"

37. "What a thrilling game—you were simply amazing!"

38. "You played your heart out and it showed—congratulations!"

39. "You kept your cool and owned that match—well done!"

40. "Watching you win today was so exciting—congrats!"

41. "You totally rocked the court—such a well-earned victory!"

42. "Every shot was perfect—you make pickleball look easy!"

43. "What an incredible match—you dominated the game!"

44. "Your skills keep getting sharper—congrats on the win!"

45. "You're unstoppable on the court—well done!"

46. "That was a brilliant match—you were on top of your game!"

47. "You played like a champion—so proud of you!"

48. "You were in complete control—what a performance!"

49. "Your victory today was beyond impressive—well done!"

50. "You brought your A-game and it totally paid off!"

51. "Congrats on another amazing win—you're incredible!"

52. "That was such a thrilling match—your talent is undeniable!"

53. "You played with so much heart—congratulations!"

54. "You were a total force out there—so proud of your win!"

55. "Your strategy was flawless—congrats on a fantastic match!"

56. "Every move was brilliant—so proud of your success!"

57. "You absolutely owned the court today—well done!"

58. "Congrats on your epic win—you make it look so fun!"

59. "You played with so much confidence and skill—fantastic job!"

60. "You were in the zone the whole time—such an awesome game!"

61. "Your energy and focus were unmatched—congrats!"

62. "You've got some serious pickleball skills—what a win!"

63. "That was an inspiring performance—congrats on your victory!"

64. "You brought so much intensity to the game—amazing work!"

65. "Congrats! Your passion for the game totally shined through!"

66. "That win was all yours—you totally earned it!"

67. "You played with such precision and power—congrats!"

68. "You're an absolute pickleball pro—what a game!"

69. "Your performance was beyond impressive—well done!"

70. "I'm in awe of how you dominated the court today—congrats!"

71. "You make every game so exciting to watch—congratulations!"

72. "Your victory today was well-deserved—you were amazing!"

73. "You played with so much heart and skill—such a fantastic match!"

74. "You totally crushed it out there—so proud of you!"

75. "That was one epic match—you're a total star!"

76. "You played like a champ—congratulations on your win!"

77. "Every move you made was spot-on—what a brilliant performance!"

78. "You played with such confidence—it was incredible to watch!"

79. "Your win today was a masterclass in pickleball!"

80. "I'm so proud of how you played—you were amazing!"

81. "You were unstoppable on the court—what a win!"

82. "Your focus and determination were off the charts—congrats!"

83. "You made that victory look effortless—well done!"

84. "Your game is on another level—such an impressive win!"

85. "You totally nailed it—what a fantastic performance!"

86. "Congrats! You're a total pickleball pro!"

87. "Your talent and hard work really showed today—congrats!"

88. "You played with such skill and heart—what a game!"

89. "You completely dominated that match—congratulations!"

90. "Your energy on the court was infectious—amazing job!"

91. "You played with so much passion—congrats on your well-earned win!"

92. "You were on fire out there—such an incredible game!"

93. "That win was all you—you played with such skill and focus!"

94. "You brought your A-game today—so proud of your victory!"

95. "What an incredible performance—you totally rocked it!"

96. "You were flawless on the court—congrats on an amazing win!"

97. "Your game today was beyond impressive—well done!"

98. "You played with such grace and confidence—what a win!"

99. "You're a total pickleball superstar—congrats!"

100. "That was an epic win—you were amazing from start to finish!"

Chapter 11

Planning Pickleball Dates

Creative Date Ideas: Beyond the Court

While the pickleball court is a fantastic place to meet and connect, planning dates beyond the game can add excitement and depth to your budding relationship. Here are some creative date ideas:

Picnic After Play: Pack a picnic basket and enjoy a meal at a nearby park after your game. This relaxed setting allows for casual conversation and the chance to unwind together while discussing the match and getting to know each other better.

Cooking Classes: Sign up for a cooking class together. This activity fosters teamwork and provides an opportunity to bond while trying something new. Plus, you'll have a delicious meal to enjoy afterward!

Visit Local Attractions: Explore nearby attractions such as museums, art galleries, or botanical gardens. This allows you to share interests and experiences outside of the court, deepening your connection.

Attend Local Events: Check out local events, such as concerts, festivals, or food fairs. Attending events together can create lasting memories and provide plenty of opportunities for conversation and fun.

Go for a Hike: If you both enjoy the outdoors, plan a hiking trip. Exploring nature together encourages meaningful conversations and can lead to shared experiences that enhance your bond.

Organizing Group Play and Social Events

Group activities can provide a comfortable way to connect with potential partners while minimizing pressure. Here's how to organize group play and social events:

Host a Social Mixer: Plan a casual social mixer for players in your local pickleball community. This could include games, refreshments, and opportunities for mingling. It's a great way to meet new people and encourage connections in a relaxed atmosphere.

Organize Tournaments: Consider organizing friendly tournaments with fellow players. These events foster camaraderie and provide ample opportunities for interaction, making it easier to connect with potential partners in a fun, competitive setting.

Plan Themed Play Days: Create themed play days (e.g., costume day, favorite color day) that encourage creativity and spark conversations. This adds an element of fun and makes it easier for players to engage with each other.

Set Up Group Outings: Organize outings that combine pickleball with other activities, such as a trip to a nearby amusement park or bowling alley. Mixing up the activities can help players relax and get to know each other in different settings.

Transitioning from Casual Play to One-on-One Dates

As you develop a connection with someone on the court, transitioning to one-on-one dates can deepen your relationship. Here are some tips for making this shift:

Gauge Interest: Pay attention to how the other person responds to your interactions. If they seem engaged and excited about spending time together, it's a positive sign that they may be open to a one-on-one date.

Make the Ask: When the time feels right, ask them directly if they'd like to go out for a coffee or dinner after a game. Keeping the invitation casual helps alleviate pressure and makes it feel more like a natural progression.

Choose a Comfortable Setting: For the first one-on-one date, choose a comfortable and relaxed environment. This could be a cozy café or a casual restaurant where you can easily talk and connect without distractions.

Follow Up on Common Interests: During your one-on-one date, reference shared experiences from the court. Discuss favorite plays, memorable matches, or aspirations in pickleball. This creates a seamless connection between your time on the court and your date.

Be Authentic: As you transition to one-on-one dates, be yourself and let your personality shine. Authenticity builds trust and creates a deeper connection, allowing both of you to feel more comfortable.

By planning creative date ideas, organizing group play and social events, and smoothly transitioning to one-on-one dates, you can create a fulfilling pickleball dating experience. Embrace the fun, nurture the connections, and enjoy every moment on and off the court!

Chapter 12

Pickleball Date Night: Planning the Perfect Evening

Once you've established a connection through pickleball, planning memorable date nights can help deepen your relationship and create lasting memories. This chapter will guide you through the essentials of organizing an exciting and engaging pickleball-themed date night, whether you're looking for something active on the court or a cozy evening off the court.

The Essentials of a Successful Pickleball Date Night

Choosing the Right Setting:

- o Depending on your partner's preferences, choose a venue that resonates with both of you. This could be a local pickleball court, a recreational center, or even your backyard if you have the space.

- o **Tip**: If you're opting for a public court, check the availability of courts in advance to avoid any disappointments.

Incorporating Fun Activities:

- o While playing pickleball is a fantastic way to connect, consider adding variety to your date. Incorporate fun activities such as mini-tournaments, skill challenges, or games that allow for playful competition.

- o **Tip**: Set up fun prizes for the winner of any games, such as a homemade treat or a fun pickleball accessory.

Mixing in Social Elements:

- o   Invite a few friends or other couples to join in on the fun! This can take the pressure off and create a more relaxed atmosphere.

- o   **Tip**: Organize a round-robin tournament or social play, allowing for mingling and light-hearted competition.

Planning Post-Game Activities:

- o   After a fun round of pickleball, consider transitioning to a more relaxed setting. This could be a picnic in the park, a casual dinner at a nearby restaurant, or even a cozy movie night at home.

- o   **Tip**: Prepare a post-game snack or meal that you both enjoy, such as healthy finger foods or your favorite pizza, to celebrate your time together.

Creating a Comfortable Atmosphere:

- o   The ambiance of your date can significantly influence your experience. Choose a comfortable setting, whether it's a cozy café, a quiet park, or your living room.

- o   **Tip**: If you're dining outdoors, bring along blankets and soft cushions for a more intimate setup under the stars.

Unique Date Night Ideas

Themed Pickleball Night:

- o   Choose a fun theme for your date night, such as a retro pickleball evening where you both dress in vintage athletic gear. It adds an element of fun and creativity to your time together.

- o **Tip**: Create a playlist of classic tunes to match your theme, enhancing the mood while you play.

Pickleball Movie Night:

- o After a day of playing, consider a movie night featuring sports-themed films or documentaries about pickleball or tennis. It's a great way to unwind and spark conversation.

- o **Tip**: Prepare some popcorn and themed snacks to keep it light and enjoyable.

Attend a Pickleball Tournament Together:

- o If there's a local tournament or exhibition happening, consider attending it together. Watching skilled players can inspire both of you and deepen your appreciation for the sport.

- o **Tip**: Engage in friendly discussions about the matches and players, sharing your thoughts and predictions.

Pickleball Picnic:

- o Combine a day of pickleball with a picnic! Pack a lunch and enjoy it at a nearby park before or after your games. It's a romantic way to relax and connect.

- o **Tip**: Bring along a portable speaker to enjoy music during your picnic, creating a festive atmosphere.

Pickleball Classes or Workshops:

Sign up for a pickleball class or workshop together. This allows you both to learn new skills while having fun and can lead to a shared passion for improvement.

Choose a class that offers playful elements or unique challenges to keep it engaging.

Final Thoughts on Planning the Perfect Pickleball Date Night

Creating the ideal pickleball date night is about blending fun, connection, and shared experiences. By thoughtfully planning activities that resonate with both of your interests, you'll not only strengthen your relationship but also enhance your love for the game. Embrace the spontaneity of pickleball and allow the thrill of the court to inspire memorable moments that transcend the sport. With the right balance of fun and romance, your pickleball date nights will be unforgettable adventures that bring you closer together.

Chapter 13

Planning Your Pickleball Getaway Outside of Your Town

Traveling outside your town provides an exciting opportunity to experience new places while indulging in your passion for pickleball. Planning a pickleball getaway outside your town can be an exhilarating experience. It allows you to immerse yourself in new surroundings while connecting with fellow pickleball enthusiasts. Here are some tips to help you select the perfect destination, balance activities, and research local pickleball facilities.

Selecting Destinations Known for Their Pickleball Culture

Identify Pickleball-Friendly Cities:

Research cities with a strong pickleball culture, such as Sun City, Arizona, or Lake Nona, Florida. These areas often host dedicated courts, clubs, and tournaments, making them ideal for your getaway.

Explore Pickleball Events and Tournaments:

Check the pickleball calendar for upcoming events or tournaments in your desired location. Participating in these events can enhance your experience and allow you to meet other players passionate about the game.

Consider Local Attractions:

Choose destinations that offer a variety of attractions beyond pickleball. Look for areas that have beautiful parks, scenic hikes, and cultural experiences to enjoy during your downtime.

Assess the Local Weather:

Weather can significantly impact your travel experience. Look for destinations with pleasant temperatures during your travel dates, ensuring optimal playing conditions.

Seek Recommendations from Fellow Players:

Connect with your local pickleball community to gather recommendations for destinations they've enjoyed. This personal insight can lead you to hidden gems that are great for pickleball enthusiasts.

Balancing Vacation Activities with Pickleball Play

Create a Balanced Itinerary:

Plan your itinerary to include a mix of pickleball and leisure activities. Dedicate specific days or time slots for games, and balance those with opportunities to explore the local area.

Prioritize Pickleball Play:

Decide how much time you want to spend on the court during your getaway. This could mean early morning games followed by sightseeing in the afternoon or dedicating full days to play.

Engage in Active Leisure Activities:

Choose active leisure activities that complement your pickleball experience. Consider options like hiking, biking, or exploring nearby parks to maintain your physical activity without overexerting yourself.

Invite Travel Companions to Play:

If traveling with friends or family, encourage them to join in on pickleball games. This adds an element of fun and togetherness, creating memories that everyone can cherish.

Capture and Share Your Experience:

Document your pickleball journey through photos and social media. Sharing your experiences can connect you with fellow players and inspire others to explore pickleball travel.

Researching Local Pickleball Clubs and Facilities Before You Go

Utilize Online Resources:

Use websites like Pickleball Central or PlayYourCourt to find local clubs and facilities in your chosen destination. These platforms often provide helpful information about available courts, amenities, and events.

Contact Local Clubs for Information:

Reach out to local pickleball clubs to inquire about their schedules, membership requirements, and any upcoming events. This will give you insight into where and when you can play.

Explore Social Media Communities:

Join local pickleball groups on social media platforms to gather tips and recommendations from fellow players. Engaging with these communities can enhance your experience and help you connect with local players.

Check for Court Availability:

Verify the availability of courts at the facilities you plan to visit. Popular locations may require reservations, so securing your spot in advance is a smart move.

Evaluate Facility Amenities:

Consider the amenities offered at the local facilities. Access to showers, restrooms, and nearby food options can significantly enhance your playing experience.

By carefully planning your pickleball getaway outside your town, you can create an enriching experience that combines your love for the sport with the thrill of exploring new destinations. With the right preparation, you'll not only enjoy exciting matches but also forge meaningful connections and create unforgettable memories on and off the court. Embrace the adventure, and may your pickleball travels be filled with fun, friendship, and the potential for romance!

Chapter 14

Navigating Challenges in Pickleball Dating

Handling Competition and Jealousy

Dating within the pickleball community can bring about feelings of competition and jealousy, especially when multiple players are vying for attention or affection. Here are some strategies for navigating these emotions:

> **Communicate Openly:** If you sense competition or jealousy, address it directly with your partner. Open communication helps clarify feelings and can diffuse tension before it escalates.

> **Celebrate Each Other's Successes:** Instead of viewing fellow players as rivals, foster a supportive atmosphere by celebrating each other's achievements on the court. Complimenting each other's skills or victories can strengthen your bond and reduce feelings of jealousy.

> **Focus on Your Unique Connection:** Remind yourselves of what makes your relationship special. Focus on your shared interests and experiences rather than comparing yourselves to others in the community.

> **Set Boundaries:** If you find that competition or jealousy is impacting your relationship negatively, establish boundaries. Agree on how much time you'll spend playing with others versus focusing on each other to ensure that both of your needs are met.

Dealing with Breakups in a Small Community

Breakups can be particularly challenging in close-knit communities like pickleball, where you may continue to encounter your ex-partner. Here are some ways to handle this situation:

> **Take Time for Yourself:** After a breakup, allow yourself time to heal and process your emotions. It's okay to step back from the pickleball scene temporarily if you need space to regroup.

Communicate with Your Ex: If you run into your ex frequently, it can be helpful to have a candid conversation about how to navigate your interactions moving forward. Agree on how to treat each other during games and events to avoid awkward situations.

Establish New Routines: Consider changing your playing times or joining different leagues temporarily to create some distance while you adjust to the breakup. This can help you establish new routines and ease any emotional discomfort.

Seek Support: Lean on friends and fellow players for support during this time. Sharing your feelings with someone who understands your situation can be invaluable as you navigate the challenges of a breakup.

Maintaining Friendships After Relationships End

One of the most delicate aspects of pickleball dating is maintaining friendships with mutual friends and acquaintances after a relationship ends. Here are some tips to help you navigate these dynamics:

Prioritize Respect: Always approach post-relationship interactions with respect for each other and the friendships involved. Avoid discussing personal details of the breakup with mutual friends, as this can create tension and discomfort.

Be Inclusive: If you're both part of the same pickleball group, make an effort to be inclusive and friendly toward one another during games. Demonstrating maturity and respect can help ease any lingering awkwardness.

Set Clear Boundaries: If maintaining a friendship feels challenging, it's okay to set boundaries with mutual friends and even your ex. Communicate your needs, and don't hesitate to take a step back from certain social situations if necessary.

Engage with the Community: Focus on building new friendships within the pickleball community. Engaging with different players can help shift your focus away from past relationships and allow you to create fresh connections.

Stay Positive: Embrace a positive mindset, acknowledging that breakups can lead to personal growth. Focusing on self-improvement and new experiences can help you move forward and maintain a healthy social life within the community.

By navigating competition and jealousy, dealing with breakups in a small community, and maintaining friendships after relationships end, you can effectively manage the challenges that arise in pickleball dating. Embrace these experiences as opportunities for growth and connection, ensuring that your journey remains enjoyable and fulfilling.

Chapter 15

Maintaining a Healthy Relationship

Balancing Love and Sport

In a relationship where both partners are passionate about pickleball, finding a balance between love and sport is essential. Here are some strategies to ensure that both aspects of your life thrive:

Set Boundaries: Establish clear boundaries around your time spent on the court and with each other. Designate specific times for pickleball practice or games, while also prioritizing quality time together away from the sport.

Enjoy Separate Activities: While it's great to share a love for pickleball, engaging in separate hobbies or interests can help maintain individuality within the relationship. This balance allows each partner to grow personally and prevents the relationship from becoming solely centered around the sport.

Plan Date Nights: Make a conscious effort to plan date nights that don't involve pickleball. Whether it's trying out a new restaurant, going for a hike, or simply enjoying a movie night at home, dedicating time to nurture your relationship outside of the sport is vital.

Celebrate Achievements Together: Take the time to celebrate both individual and shared accomplishments. Whether it's winning a match or achieving a personal goal, acknowledging each other's successes helps reinforce the importance of both love and sport in your lives.

Communication Strategies for Active Couples

Effective communication is key to maintaining a healthy relationship, especially when both partners are actively involved in a sport like pickleball. Here are some strategies to enhance communication:

Schedule Check-Ins: Regularly schedule check-ins to discuss your relationship, your goals, and any concerns you may have. This practice helps create an open line of communication and allows both partners to voice their feelings in a structured environment.

Use "I" Statements: When discussing sensitive topics or addressing concerns, use "I" statements to express how you feel. This approach fosters understanding and reduces the likelihood of defensiveness. For example, instead of saying, "You never support my games," try, "I feel unsupported when I don't see you at my matches."

Practice Active Listening: Focus on listening to your partner without interrupting or formulating a response while they speak. Reflect back what you hear to ensure mutual understanding and validate each other's feelings.

Share Goals and Aspirations: Openly discuss your individual and shared goals, both in pickleball and life. Supporting each other's aspirations strengthens the relationship and encourages teamwork on and off the court.

Be Honest and Vulnerable: Foster an environment of trust by being honest and vulnerable with each other. Sharing your fears, frustrations, and dreams deepens emotional intimacy and helps navigate challenges together.

Supporting Each Other's Growth in the Game and in Life

Supporting each other's growth is crucial for a healthy relationship, especially in a sport-centered partnership. Here are some ways to nurture each other's development:

Encourage Skill Development: Actively support your partner in improving their pickleball skills. Attend their practices, offer constructive feedback, or practice together to help each other grow as players.

Set Shared Goals: Work together to establish shared goals, both in pickleball and in life. Whether it's participating in a tournament or pursuing a career milestone, having common objectives fosters teamwork and unity.

Celebrate Progress: Acknowledge and celebrate each other's progress, whether big or small. Celebrating milestones helps build confidence and reinforces the idea that you're both invested in each other's growth.

Provide Emotional Support: Be there for your partner during tough matches or challenging times. Offering encouragement and emotional support can make a significant difference in how both partners navigate the ups and downs of both sport and life.

Promote a Healthy Lifestyle: Encourage healthy habits that benefit both your pickleball performance and overall well-being. This can include exercising together, maintaining a balanced diet, and prioritizing rest and recovery.

By focusing on maintaining a healthy relationship through balancing love and sport, implementing effective communication strategies, and supporting each other's growth, couples can thrive both on and off the pickleball court. Embracing the journey together enhances not only their game but also their connection, leading to a fulfilling partnership grounded in love and shared passions.

Chapter 16

Strengthening Your Relationship Through Pickleball

The Importance of Teamwork

In any relationship, teamwork is essential, and pickleball provides an excellent opportunity to cultivate this skill. Playing doubles or participating in team events encourages collaboration and fosters a sense of partnership. Learn how to strategize together, support each other during matches, and celebrate victories as a unit. This collaborative spirit can enhance your bond and build trust, both on and off the court.

Setting Shared Goals

Establishing common goals within your relationship can lead to greater satisfaction and connection. Whether it's improving your skills, participating in tournaments, or even engaging in social events as a couple, setting shared goals helps align your interests and aspirations. Work together to identify what you want to achieve and create a plan to support each other along the way.

Overcoming Challenges Together

Every relationship faces challenges, and pickleball is no different. Whether it's dealing with competition, injuries, or external pressures, approaching these hurdles as a united front strengthens your relationship. Communicate openly about your feelings and work together to find solutions. Embracing challenges can lead to growth, resilience, and a deeper appreciation for one another.

Celebrating Milestones

Celebrate each milestone, both big and small, in your pickleball journey and relationship. Whether it's a personal best in a match, an anniversary, or reaching a new level in your game, take the time to acknowledge these achievements. Celebrating milestones reinforces your commitment to each other and creates lasting memories that enhance your connection.

Expanding Your Social Circle

Engaging in pickleball also allows you to expand your social circle. Invite friends to join you on the court or participate in community events together. Building a supportive network of friends can enrich your relationship and provide additional opportunities for socializing. The more you engage with others, the more your relationship can flourish in a vibrant community atmosphere.

Growing together through pickleball is a rewarding journey that combines the excitement of the sport with the nurturing of your relationship. By embracing teamwork, setting shared goals, overcoming challenges, celebrating milestones, and expanding your social circle, you can create a strong, lasting bond. As you navigate your pickleball dating adventure, remember that every serve and rally is an opportunity to deepen your connection and enjoy the beautiful game together.

Chapter 17

Case Studies in Pickleball Dating

Understanding the dynamics of dating within the pickleball community can enhance your experience and help you forge meaningful connections. Here are some case studies that highlight effective strategies and common pitfalls in pickleball dating:

Case Study 1: The Matchmaker

Scenario: They both played at a local pickleball league and regularly participated in social events. Their shared interest in the sport allowed them to get to know each other over time.

What to Do:

Be Approachable: She often smiled and initiated conversations after matches, making it easy for him to feel comfortable approaching her.

Show Enthusiasm: He frequently expressed his love for pickleball and shared tips, which sparked engaging discussions.

Participate in Group Activities: They joined group outings, such as tournaments or social play events, where they could bond outside of formal matches.

What Not to Do:

Avoid Playing Hard to Get: Initially, he hesitated to ask her out, thinking it might seem too forward. However, when he finally asked her to grab a drink after a game, it strengthened their connection.

Don't Neglect Other Friendships: He ensured he maintained friendships with other players, avoiding the perception of being overly focused on her, which kept things light and friendly.

Case Study 2: The Competitive Edge

Scenario: They met at a pickleball tournament where they were both competing. The competitive atmosphere heightened their interest in each other.

What to Do:

> Encourage Each Other: After each match, he congratulated her on her performance, which created a supportive environment.

> Find Common Ground: They discovered shared interests beyond pickleball, such as hiking and travel, during their discussions.

> Keep It Light: They made jokes about their competitive nature, which diffused any tension and made their interactions fun.

What Not to Do:

> Avoid Intimidation: He initially played too aggressively, which made her feel intimidated. He quickly realized that a collaborative approach to the game would foster a better connection.

> Don't Overanalyze Matches: After one particularly tough match, she fixated on her performance, which negatively affected her mood. Instead, focusing on enjoying the game together would have kept the mood light.

Case Study 3: The Friendship Zone

Scenario: They became close friends through their pickleball group but had different romantic interests.

What to Do:

> Communicate Openly: He expressed his feelings to her but respected her decision when she indicated she wasn't interested in dating.

> Maintain the Friendship: They both continued to support each other's games and social activities without awkwardness.

What Not to Do:

Avoid Mixed Signals: he occasionally flirted, leading her to question his intentions. Clear communication helped avoid misunderstandings.

Don't Let Feelings Interfere: After he shared his feelings, he made an effort not to let it affect their friendship, ensuring their bond remained strong.

Case Study 4: The Unexpected Connection

Scenario: They met at a community pickleball clinic. Their initial connection was sparked by a shared struggle to learn the game.

What to Do:

Encourage Each Other: They bonded over their beginner status and encouraged each other to improve, building a supportive relationship.

Plan Casual Outings: After the clinic, they organized casual practices and outings, which allowed them to get to know each other better in a low-pressure setting.

What Not to Do:

Avoid Overthinking: She initially worried that her lack of skills might deter him. Instead, embracing their shared learning experience allowed them to connect more deeply.

Don't Rush into Seriousness: They focused on having fun without the pressure of a romantic relationship, which allowed their feelings to develop naturally over time.

Case Study 5: The Social Butterfly

Scenario: She was a familiar face at pickleball socials, known for her vivacious and outgoing nature. She was eager to find a special connection within the pickleball community.

What to Do:

> Be Inclusive: She actively welcomed newcomers into conversations and games, fostering a friendly atmosphere that made it easy for potential partners to engage.

> Be Authentic: Her genuine approach to interactions attracted others, helping her establish connections grounded in shared interests and mutual respect.

What Not to Do:

> Avoid Favoritism: Although she enjoyed chatting with various players, she was careful not to single out one person too early, preventing feelings of jealousy among her peers.

> Don't Share Too Much Too Soon: In her enthusiasm to build connections, she sometimes revealed personal information too quickly. By focusing on gradual rapport-building, she enhanced the depth of her relationships.

Case Study 6: The Competitive Spirit

Scenario: He was a highly competitive pickleball player who loved the thrill of matches. He was on the lookout for someone who could match his energy on the court.

What to Do:

> Embrace Healthy Competition: He invited potential partners to play together, framing matches as fun challenges rather than intense competitions. This approach made the experience enjoyable for both parties.

> Celebrate Others' Wins: He made it a point to congratulate opponents and partners on their successes, fostering a supportive atmosphere that encouraged camaraderie.

What Not to Do:

> Don't Take It Too Seriously: While competitiveness is part of the game, he avoided being overly serious about wins and losses, as this could intimidate potential dates.

> Avoid Neglecting Social Aspects: He ensured that he balanced his competitive nature with socializing off the court, so that potential partners could see his fun and approachable side.

Case Study 7: The Newbie

Scenario: She had just started playing pickleball and was eager to learn the game while also hoping to meet new people.

What to Do:

> Ask for Help: She was open about being a beginner, asking for tips and advice from more experienced players. This not only helped her improve but also initiated conversations.

> Join Beginner Classes: She signed up for beginner classes where she could meet others at her skill level, creating a comfortable environment for socializing.

What Not to Do:

> Don't Be Shy to Engage: She initially hesitated to join group conversations, which made it harder to connect. She learned to overcome this shyness to meet new people.

> Avoid Comparing Yourself to Others: She realized that comparing her skills to seasoned players discouraged her. Instead, she focused on enjoying her own progress and journey.

Case Study 8: The Committed Player

Scenario: He was a devoted pickleball enthusiast who played regularly and was looking for someone who shared his passion for the sport.

What to Do:

> Share Passion: He frequently shared updates about his pickleball matches and tournaments, inviting others to join and participate. This made it easier for others to relate to his enthusiasm.

> Be Open to New Connections: He engaged in conversations with various players, expressing genuine interest in their experiences with the sport.

What Not to Do:

> Don't Limit Your Circle: While he preferred to play with experienced players, he avoided excluding beginners, understanding that everyone's passion for the sport is valuable.

> Avoid Being Overly Competitive: He maintained a friendly demeanor during games, ensuring that his competitive spirit didn't overshadow the social aspect of the game.

Case Study 9: The Social Connector

Scenario: She was known as the social connector within her pickleball community, often introducing friends to new players and fostering connections.

What to Do:

> Host Events: She organized casual pickleball get-togethers, encouraging her friends and acquaintances to bring along potential dates. This created a relaxed environment for mingling.

> Encourage Group Play: She promoted group play to break the ice and help people feel more comfortable around each other.

What Not to Do:

> Don't Play Matchmaker: While she loved connecting others, she avoided forcing chemistry between players, understanding that connections should happen naturally.

> Avoid Neglecting Her Own Game: In focusing on helping others connect, she ensured she still prioritized her own game and practice to maintain her skills.

Case Study 10: The Fitness Enthusiast

Scenario: He was a fitness enthusiast who used pickleball as part of his active lifestyle and was looking for someone who shared similar values.

What to Do:

> Promote Wellness: He often talked about the benefits of staying active, sharing workout tips and healthy lifestyle choices with potential partners.

> Suggest Fitness Dates: He proposed pickleball as a fun fitness date idea, showcasing the blend of activity and enjoyment.

What Not to Do:

> Don't Be Overbearing: While he was passionate about fitness, he made sure not to pressure others into a strict regimen, promoting a balanced approach instead.

> Avoid Exclusivity: He refrained from only seeking out players who were exceptionally fit, recognizing that everyone's fitness journey is unique and valuable.

Navigating the pickleball dating scene can be an exciting adventure filled with opportunities for genuine connections. By learning from these case studies, you can understand what behaviors foster successful relationships and which actions to avoid. Whether you're aiming for love, friendship, or a little of both, remember to keep the joy of the game at the forefront of your journey. Embrace the social aspects of pickleball, and enjoy the moments spent both on and off the court!

Chapter 18

Navigating Relationship Dynamics on and off the Court

In the realm of pickleball dating, the dynamics of your relationship can shift as you progress from casual games to deeper connections. Understanding these dynamics and navigating them with care is essential for fostering lasting relationships. This chapter explores the various relationship stages that can develop within the pickleball community and offers strategies for maintaining a healthy balance between sport and romance.

Understanding Relationship Stages in Pickleball Dating

The Initial Connection:

This stage is characterized by meeting new players and sparking interest through casual play. It's important to keep things light and fun while gauging mutual attraction.

Tip: Focus on building rapport through shared experiences on the court, such as teaming up for doubles or participating in social events.

Building Friendship:

As you connect with someone, your relationship may deepen into a friendship. This is a great time to engage in off-court activities, such as joining a local league or attending pickleball socials together.

Tip: Cultivate your friendship by sharing your passion for the sport while also exploring common interests outside of pickleball.

Transitioning to Romance:

When the friendship evolves into romantic interest, it's crucial to communicate openly about your feelings. Look for opportunities to express your interest in a more personal setting.

Tip: Plan one-on-one pickleball dates that provide a relaxed atmosphere for discussing your feelings and aspirations.

Navigating Challenges:

Every relationship faces challenges, especially when navigating the competitive nature of pickleball. Differences in skill level or competitive spirit can lead to tension if not managed carefully.

Tip: Emphasize teamwork and support during games, celebrating each other's strengths and encouraging growth.

Strengthening the Bond:

As your relationship becomes more established, continue to prioritize communication and quality time, both on and off the court. Engage in activities that strengthen your bond, such as practicing together or attending tournaments.

Tip: Create shared goals related to your pickleball journey, like improving specific skills or participating in local competitions.

Maintaining Balance Between Sport and Romance

Setting Boundaries:

Establish clear boundaries to differentiate between your sports life and your romantic life. This prevents misunderstandings and keeps the relationship healthy.

Tip: Discuss expectations regarding playing together and participating in tournaments, ensuring both partners feel comfortable.

Encouraging Individual Growth:

While growing as a couple is important, it's equally vital to encourage each other's individual pursuits. Support your partner's journey in improving their skills or pursuing other interests.

Tip: Take time apart to play with other partners or engage in separate activities, allowing for personal growth.

Fostering Open Communication:

Honest communication is the cornerstone of any healthy relationship. Discuss any concerns or feelings about your pickleball experiences together, ensuring both partners feel heard.

Tip: Schedule regular check-ins to discuss your relationship, both in terms of sports and personal aspects, fostering transparency.

Celebrating Milestones Together:

Celebrate achievements in pickleball and personal milestones as a couple. Recognizing these moments strengthens your bond and enhances your shared experiences.

Tip: Host a small celebration after a successful tournament or a personal accomplishment, creating lasting memories together.

Navigating Breakups Gracefully:

If a relationship doesn't work out, it's important to handle breakups with maturity, especially in a close-knit community like pickleball. Maintain respect for each other and the sport.

Tip: Allow space for healing and avoid discussing the breakup openly in group settings. Focus on remaining friends if possible and prioritize the joy of playing the game you both love.

Navigating relationship dynamics within the pickleball community can be both rewarding and challenging. By understanding the stages of relationship development, maintaining a healthy balance between sport and romance, and fostering open communication, you can create a fulfilling partnership that thrives on and off the court. As you continue your pickleball dating journey, remember to embrace the joy of connecting with others through shared passions, creating lasting memories and meaningful relationships.

Chapter 19

Why Boomers Love Pickleball

In recent years, a new phenomenon has swept across the United States, captivating the hearts of many Baby Boomers: pickleball. This dynamic paddle sport, a blend of tennis, badminton, and ping-pong, has not only revived the competitive spirit in many but has also created a vibrant community for social interaction and romance. The allure of pickleball lies in its accessibility, social dynamics, and the joyful energy it brings to its players, allowing Boomers to reconnect with their athleticism and forge meaningful connections—both platonic and romantic.

Rediscovering Physical Activity

For many Baby Boomers, the transition into retirement has provided a unique opportunity to reevaluate their lifestyles, particularly regarding physical activity. After decades of work and family responsibilities, many are seeking ways to stay active, fit, and healthy. Pickleball serves as an excellent choice for several reasons:

> Accessibility: Unlike traditional racquet sports that can be physically demanding, pickleball is relatively easy to learn and play. The smaller court size and slower pace make it suitable for players of varying skill levels and physical abilities.

> Low Impact: As Boomers become more conscious of joint health, pickleball offers a low-impact workout that minimizes stress on the knees and hips compared to more intense sports.

> Social Engagement: Many Boomers are drawn to the social aspects of pickleball. The game encourages camaraderie and teamwork, allowing players to form friendships and engage in social activities beyond the court.

> The Social Side of Pickleball: The social nature of pickleball creates a welcoming environment for players, making it an ideal setting for meeting new people and nurturing relationships. Here are several ways pickleball fosters social connections:

Community: Pickleball clubs and recreational centers often host regular games, tournaments, and social events. These gatherings provide opportunities for players to meet others with similar interests and build friendships.

Mixed-Ability Play: Unlike some sports where competition can be fierce, pickleball often emphasizes inclusivity. Players of different skill levels can compete together, creating a friendly atmosphere conducive to mingling.

Team Play: Many Boomers find joy in partnering up for doubles matches. This cooperative aspect allows players to bond while developing teamwork skills, enhancing the sense of connection.

Finding Romance Through Pickleball

As Boomers engage in the world of pickleball, many find that it not only revives their interest in physical activity but also sparks romantic connections. Numerous Boomers have shared their positive experiences with pickleball, highlighting not just the physical benefits but also the newfound connections and relationships they've fostered through the game.

Here's how pickleball can serve as a catalyst for love:

Shared Interests: Meeting someone who shares a love for pickleball provides a solid foundation for a relationship. The shared activity creates a common ground, making it easier to connect and bond over mutual interests.

Natural Chemistry: The playful, competitive nature of the sport can lead to flirtation and camaraderie. As players engage in friendly competition, they often find themselves laughing and sharing playful banter, which can lead to deeper connections.

Social Events: Pickleball tournaments and social events often include opportunities for singles to mingle. These gatherings create a relaxed atmosphere where potential romantic partners can interact without the pressure of traditional dating scenarios.

Health and Vitality: Engaging in physical activity can boost confidence and self-esteem, making individuals feel more attractive and open to new relationships. The active lifestyle associated with pickleball can enhance one's overall well-being, making dating and socializing more enjoyable.

Pickleball is more than just a sport; it's a transformative experience for many Baby Boomers seeking to reignite their passions for physical activity and connection. As they navigate this vibrant community, they often find not only fitness but also friendship and love. The accessibility, social engagement, and playful nature of pickleball make it an ideal avenue for Boomers to rediscover their zest for life—both on and off the court. Whether they are swinging paddles or forming romantic connections, the pickleball court has become a new frontier for Baby Boomers looking to embrace an active and fulfilling lifestyle.

Chapter 20
Real-Life Success Stories

Couples Who Met Through Pickleball: Their Journeys

The pickleball community has brought together many couples who have found love and companionship on and off the court. Here are a few inspiring stories that highlight their journeys:

The Pickleball Pair

After retiring, one individual discovered a local pickleball league and decided to join. During their first few games, they met another player with a similar passion for sports. Their shared love for pickleball blossomed into a romantic relationship, and they now spend weekends playing together and traveling to tournaments.

The Resilient Couple

Following the loss of a spouse, one individual felt lonely and sought connection by joining a pickleball club. There, they encountered a welcoming group of players. Through the sport, they forged new friendships and eventually found companionship in a fellow player, leading to a loving relationship filled with adventure and joy.

The Competitive Couple

They met at a local pickleball league. Initially, they bonded over their shared love for the game, often teaming up for mixed doubles matches. As they played together week after week, their chemistry blossomed into romance. They now play competitively together and even host weekly game nights for their friends, fostering a lively and fun pickleball community.

The Casual Companions

Their love story began during a charity pickleball tournament. They were paired together randomly, and their playful banter and supportive teamwork caught the attention of those around them. After the tournament, they started going on casual outings to local cafes and eventually became inseparable. Their mutual passion for pickleball continues to strengthen their relationship, with plans to travel together for national tournaments.

The Rival Romantics

Their relationship started as a friendly rivalry on the court. They often competed against each other during league matches, exchanging playful trash talk and good-natured competitiveness. Over time, they developed a deeper connection and began dating. Their relationship has been enriched by their friendly competition, leading to joint training sessions and mutual encouragement to improve their skills.

The Hawaiian Connection

While attending a conference in Hawaii, she discovered a local pickleball group and joined a match on her last day. There, she met him—a friendly local player who invited her to team up. Their shared love for the sport sparked an instant connection, and they exchanged contact information after a fun day on the court.

As they kept in touch through video calls, they began visiting each other's cities, playing pickleball and exploring together. Competing in tournaments strengthened their bond, allowing them to navigate challenges and celebrate wins as a team.

Eventually, they made a commitment to each other and established a shared home base, balancing their careers with their passion for pickleball. Now, they spend their days coaching youth leagues and planning adventures, proving that love can flourish in unexpected places when fueled by shared interests.

The Adventurous Duo

They met at a pickleball clinic aimed at beginners and quickly realized they shared more than just a love for the game. Their initial encounters on the court led to hiking trips and biking adventures off the court. Now, they balance their love for pickleball with outdoor escapades, often exploring new locations together while participating in pickleball tournaments.

The Social Sweethearts

This couple connected at a community pickleball social event. Their shared enthusiasm for mingling and meeting new people helped them forge a quick friendship that blossomed into romance. They often host mixers and social events for their local pickleball community, enjoying the dual benefit of building connections and deepening their relationship.

The Long-Distance Lovers

Having met through an online pickleball forum, they first bonded over strategy discussions and tips. Eventually, they decided to meet in person at a regional tournament, where sparks flew during their matches together. They now make regular trips to see each other and plan to play together at various tournaments, making the most of their shared love for the sport.

The Fitness Friends

After joining a pickleball boot camp, they started as workout buddies. Their shared goals of improving their game and staying active led to friendly matches and training sessions. As they encouraged each other on the court, their bond grew stronger, evolving into a romantic relationship that emphasizes health, fitness, and fun.

The Spontaneous Pair

They met at a last-minute pickleball game when both were seeking players to fill in. Their spontaneous match turned into an unforgettable day of laughter and friendly competition. They continued playing together, developing a close-knit relationship full of surprise outings and impromptu adventures, always seeking the next pickleball challenge together.

The Community Champions

This couple met while volunteering at a local pickleball event, where they bonded over their shared passion for giving back to the community. Their love for the sport and desire to make a difference in their local area led them to create their own pickleball charity tournaments. Their partnership is built on love, community, and teamwork, inspiring others to get involved in the sport.

The Family Focused Team

Having met through a pickleball league that welcomed families, they found common ground in their love for the sport and parenting. As they enjoyed matches with their kids, they grew closer and eventually began dating. They now play as a family, taking turns in doubles matches while instilling a love for pickleball in their children.

The Pilot and the Pickleball Partner

She met him at an open play session, where he played pickleball between flights as a pilot. Seeking a morning partner, he connected with her, and her remote job allowed them to play together regularly.

Their shared love for the game quickly turned into something more. After matches, they enjoyed breakfast and shared stories, deepening their bond. As their skills improved on the court, so did their romance, transforming playful rivalry into a supportive partnership. Together, they embraced a lifestyle filled with adventure and laughter, proving that love can flourish in unexpected places.

Lessons Learned and Advice from Successful Pickleball Daters

The experiences of couples who have successfully navigated the pickleball dating scene offer valuable insights for others seeking love. Here are some key lessons learned and advice from these couples:

Stay Open-Minded: Many successful couples emphasize the importance of being open to meeting new people. Even if you have a specific type in mind, allowing yourself to connect with different personalities can lead to unexpected matches.

Prioritize Communication: Open and honest communication is crucial for any relationship. Couples recommend discussing boundaries, feelings, and expectations early on to foster trust and understanding.

Embrace the Fun: Successful daters stress the importance of keeping things light and enjoyable. Engaging in playful banter, sharing laughter on the court, and not taking the game too seriously can help build strong connections.

Participate in Group Activities: Many couples suggest participating in group outings and social events to ease the pressure of one-on-one dates. This creates a relaxed atmosphere where connections can develop naturally.

Support Each Other's Goals: Supporting your partner's goals— whether on or off the court—strengthens the bond and enhances teamwork. Celebrate each other's successes and encourage one another in both pickleball and personal endeavors.

The Role of Community in Building Lasting Relationships

The pickleball community plays a significant role in nurturing lasting relationships. Here's how the community contributes to successful dating experiences:

Shared Interests: Being part of a community that shares a common interest in pickleball creates an instant connection. Couples often find that their shared passion serves as a strong foundation for their relationship.

Social Support: The pickleball community offers a supportive network of friends and fellow players who can provide encouragement and guidance throughout the dating process. Having a strong support system can make navigating relationships easier and more enjoyable.

Opportunities for Connection: The structured nature of leagues, tournaments, and social events provides numerous opportunities for individuals to meet and connect. This environment fosters natural interactions that can lead to romantic relationships.

Building Friendships First: Many couples find that forming friendships within the community first helps establish a solid foundation for romantic relationships. This allows for organic growth and helps both partners feel comfortable and secure.

Creating Lasting Memories: Shared experiences within the community—whether through friendly matches, social gatherings, or tournaments—help couples create lasting memories together. These shared moments deepen the emotional bond and enhance the relationship.

Exploring real-life success stories and lessons from pickleball daters, along with understanding the community's role, provides inspiration for navigating your own pickleball dating journey. Embracing the game while forging meaningful connections can lead to fulfilling relationships that thrive on and off the court.

Chapter 21

Embrace the Game and Love

The Joy of Combining Passion with Romance

Finding love through pickleball is not just about the game; it's about the joy of merging your passions with your romantic endeavors. The thrill of engaging rallies, the adrenaline of competitive matches, and the camaraderie of tournaments all serve to create a unique bonding experience that can deepen connections and enhance your relationships. When you share a passion for pickleball with someone special, you establish a foundation built on mutual interests and excitement.

This combination of love and sport fosters not only camaraderie but also intimacy, transforming each moment on the court into something extraordinary. The laughter shared over a playful game, the encouragement exchanged during intense rallies, and the celebrations of victories—big or small—create memories that can solidify your connection. Pickleball has the incredible ability to break down barriers and forge bonds that can lead to lasting partnerships. It's an invitation to connect on a level that transcends mere physical attraction, diving deeper into shared experiences that enrich both your game and your life.

Encouragement to Dive into the Pickleball Dating Scene

If you're considering exploring the pickleball dating scene, now is the perfect time to dive in! The pickleball community is vibrant, inclusive, and welcoming, offering numerous opportunities to meet new people who share your interests. Whether you're a seasoned player or just starting out, embracing the fun of the game can lead to unexpected connections and delightful encounters.

Join local leagues, participate in social events, or simply show up at community courts. Engage with fellow players—share tips, offer support, or challenge each other to friendly matches. Each interaction is an opportunity to not only improve your game but also to build meaningful relationships. Allow yourself the freedom to explore connections that could lead to lasting love. Remember, every match is a chance to discover not just a partner but also a friend.

Pickleball provides a unique platform for forming friendships that could blossom into something more profound. As you navigate the dating scene, keep your heart open to the possibilities that come your way, whether it's a friendly rivalry or a romantic connection.

Final Thoughts on Finding Love on the Court

As you embark on your journey to find love on the court, keep an open heart and an open mind. Embrace the spirit of pickleball, where fun meets competition, and where the lines between friendship and romance often blur. The experiences shared with others who share your passion for pickleball can lead to meaningful relationships that extend far beyond the game.

Take note of the lessons learned along the way. Every missed shot, every victory, and every moment of laughter contributes to your growth, both as a player and as a person. The friendships formed on the court can offer support and encouragement as you navigate the complexities of dating, and they can become an invaluable part of your journey.

Through pickleball, you'll find opportunities to connect with others, to share stories, and to create lasting memories. The potential for love exists in every serve and volley, waiting to be discovered. With each match played, you're not just participating in a sport; you're crafting the potential for a beautiful romance that flourishes in both the game and in life.

So, lace up your shoes, grab your paddle, and head to the court with enthusiasm! Embrace the joy of the game and allow it to guide you toward the love you seek. Whether you find that special someone during a thrilling match or while cheering on friends at a tournament, remember that love is often found where you least expect it—right there on the court, where passion and play intertwine.

Chapter 22

Top Pickleball Clubs and Courts Across U.S. Cities

This list covers a variety of locations across the U.S. with a mix of public, private, and community-based pickleball clubs and courts. Whether you're looking for a casual game or competitive play, these destinations offer a range of opportunities for pickleball enthusiasts!

New York City, NY

Central Park Pickleball Courts

Location: North Meadow Recreation Center, Central Park, New York, NY 10024

Outdoor public courts available.

West Side YMCA Pickleball

Address: 5 W 63rd St, New York, NY 10023

Indoor pickleball courts with membership access.

Los Angeles, CA

Playa Vista Pickleball Courts

Address: 13196 Bluff Creek Dr, Playa Vista, CA 90094

Outdoor courts in a popular neighborhood park.

Westchester Pickleball Club

Address: 7000 W Manchester Ave, Los Angeles, CA 90045

A private club offering clinics and tournaments.

Chicago, IL

North Avenue Beach Pickleball Courts

Address: 1600 N Lake Shore Dr, Chicago, IL 60614

Outdoor pickleball courts near the lakefront.

Waveland Pickleball Club

Address: 3700 N Recreation Dr, Chicago, IL 60613

Community pickleball club offering league play and social events.

Houston, TX

Memorial Park Pickleball Courts

Address: 1500 E Memorial Loop Dr, Houston, TX 77007

Popular outdoor public courts with ample space.

Tomball Pickleball Club

Address: 700 E Main St, Tomball, TX 77375

Indoor and outdoor courts available for club members.

Phoenix, AZ

Pinnacle Peak Park

Address: 26802 N 102nd St, Scottsdale, AZ 85262

Outdoor courts surrounded by beautiful desert scenery.

Indian School Park & Tennis Center

Address: 4289 N Hayden Rd, Scottsdale, AZ 85251

Features multiple outdoor pickleball courts with a regular schedule of play.

San Diego, CA

Balboa Park Pickleball Courts

Address: 2221 Morley Field Dr, San Diego, CA 92104

Well-known outdoor courts located in a central park setting.

La Jolla Pickleball Club

Address: 8301 Nautilus St, La Jolla, CA 92037

Private club offering regular pickleball games and events.

Seattle, WA

Green Lake Park Pickleball Courts

Address: 7201 E Green Lake Dr N, Seattle, WA 98115

A popular outdoor public court with scenic views.

Magnuson Park Pickleball Courts

Address: 7400 Sand Point Way NE, Seattle, WA 98115

Outdoor courts near the waterfront with plenty of space for casual and competitive play.

Miami, FL

Flamingo Park Tennis Center

Address: 1200 Meridian Ave, Miami Beach, FL 33139

Outdoor pickleball courts in a well-known park, near South Beach.

Key Biscayne Community Center

Address: 10 Village Green Way, Key Biscayne, FL 33149

Indoor courts available for members of the community.

Denver, CO

Central Park Pickleball Courts

Address: 9651 E Martin Luther King Jr Blvd, Denver, CO 80238

A popular outdoor destination for pickleball in Denver.

Wash Park Pickleball Club

Address: 701 S Franklin St, Denver, CO 80209

Community club with access to both indoor and outdoor courts.

Nashville, TN

Centennial Sportsplex

Address: 222 25th Ave N, Nashville, TN 37203

Indoor and outdoor courts available for community play.

Sevier Park Pickleball Courts

Address: 3021 Lealand Ln, Nashville, TN 37204

Outdoor courts in a scenic neighborhood park.

Austin, TX

Austin Tennis & Pickleball Center

Address: 7800 Johnny Morris Rd, Austin, TX 78724

Offers a large number of outdoor courts for both tennis and pickleball.

Bouldin Acres Pickleball

Address: 2027 S Lamar Blvd, Austin, TX 78704

A social space offering food, drinks, and pickleball courts for casual play.

Portland, OR

Sellwood Park Pickleball Courts

Address: SE 7th Ave and Miller St, Portland, OR 97202

Popular outdoor pickleball courts for casual and competitive play.

Eastmoreland Racquet Club

Address: 3015 SE Berkeley Pl, Portland, OR 97202

Offers indoor pickleball with clinics and league play.

Orlando, FL

Barnett Park Pickleball Courts

Address: 4801 W Colonial Dr, Orlando, FL 32808

Outdoor courts with regular open play sessions.

Fort Gatlin Recreation Complex

Address: 2009 Lake Margaret Dr, Orlando, FL 32806

Indoor courts available for both members and drop-ins.

Atlanta, GA

Shady Valley Park

Address: 2700 Shady Valley Dr NE, Atlanta, GA 30324

Offers a well-maintained outdoor pickleball court in a scenic park.

Bobby Jones Golf Course and Pickleball Courts

Address: 2205 Northside Dr NW, Atlanta, GA 30305

Offers multiple pickleball courts and access to a clubhouse.

Las Vegas, NV

Durango Hills Park Pickleball Courts

Address: 3521 N Durango Dr, Las Vegas, NV 89129

Popular outdoor courts with a view of the Las Vegas mountains.

Sunset Park Pickleball Courts

Address: 2601 E Sunset Rd, Las Vegas, NV 89120

Offers a large number of outdoor courts for players of all skill levels.

Chapter 23

International Pickleball Clubs

Pickleball is rapidly gaining popularity internationally, emerging as one of the fastest-growing sports across the globe. Originating in the United States in the 1960s, the sport has expanded its reach, with numerous countries establishing national organizations and clubs dedicated to promoting pickleball. Nations such as Canada, the United Kingdom, Australia, and Brazil have embraced the game, hosting tournaments and fostering local communities. The establishment of the International Federation of Pickleball (IFP) has further facilitated global growth, uniting players and governing bodies to standardize rules and promote international competitions. As more people discover the sport's accessibility and social aspects, pickleball is poised for continued expansion, attracting enthusiasts of all ages and skill levels worldwide.

These clubs and organizations are instrumental in promoting and expanding the reach of pickleball around the world, making it easier for players to connect and enjoy the sport!

Here's a list of international pickleball clubs where players can join and participate in the growing global pickleball community:

Pickleball Canada

Location: Canada

Description: The governing body for pickleball in Canada, promoting the sport through clubs and tournaments across the country.

Website: www.pickleballcanada.org

Canadian Pickleball Association

Location: Canada

Description: A national organization that promotes and develops pickleball in Canada through coaching, competition, and club resources.

Website: www.canadianpickleball.com

British Pickleball Association

Location: United Kingdom

Description: The national governing body for pickleball in England, Scotland, and Wales, providing resources and organizing events.

Website: www.pickleballengland.org

Pickleball Australia

Location: Australia

Description: A national association promoting the sport of pickleball through local clubs and tournaments across Australia.

Website: www.pickleballaus.org

International Federation of Pickleball (IFP)

Location: Global

Description: A worldwide organization that governs the sport of pickleball, supporting member nations and promoting international play.

Website: www.ifpickleball.org

Pickleball Spain

Location: Spain

Description: A community for pickleball enthusiasts in Spain, promoting clubs, events, and player connections across the country.

Website: www.pickleballspain.org

Pickleball Singapore

Location: Singapore

Description: The official organization for pickleball in Singapore, facilitating local clubs and tournaments for players.

Website: www.pickleball.sg

Pickleball New Zealand

Location: New Zealand

Description: The national body for pickleball in New Zealand, providing support and resources for clubs and players across the country.

Website: www.pickleballnz.org.nz

European Pickleball Association

Location: Europe

Description: A governing body that oversees and promotes the growth of pickleball in Europe through various member countries.

Website: www.europeanpickleball.org

Pickleball Brazil

Location: Brazil

Description: A growing community focused on promoting pickleball through clubs, tournaments, and events throughout Brazil.

Website: www.pickleballbrazil.org

Chapter 24
International Pickleball Clubs

These online groups provide a great way to connect with the pickleball community, improve your game, and stay updated on the latest events!

Facebook Groups

Pickleball Forum

Description: One of the largest online pickleball communities with over 80,000 members. Players discuss strategies, equipment, and tournaments.

Website: www.facebook.com/groups/pickleballforum

Pickleball Community

Description: A friendly group for players to share experiences, ask questions, and find pickleball partners.

Website: www.facebook.com/groups/pickleballcommunity

Pickleball Central Players Group

Description: A community run by Pickleball Central, focused on equipment advice, discounts, and player connections.

Website: www.facebook.com/groups/pickleballcentral

Women's Pickleball Network

Description: A space dedicated to female pickleball players for support, networking, and organizing meetups.

Website: www.facebook.com/groups/womenspickleballnetwork

Pickleball Enthusiasts

Description: Open to all skill levels, this group focuses on growing the sport and sharing playing tips.

Website: www.facebook.com/groups/pickleballenthusiasts

Reddit Communities

r/Pickleball

Description: A growing subreddit with discussions about strategy, court etiquette, gear recommendations, and upcoming events.

Website: www.reddit.com/r/pickleball

r/PickleballWorld

Description: A subreddit for players around the world to connect, share experiences, and learn about international pickleball events.

Website: www.reddit.com/r/PickleballWorld

Pickleball-Specific Online Platforms

PickleballTournaments.com

Description: A website with an active community forum for tournament discussions, registration, and player matchmaking.

Website: www.pickleballtournaments.com

The Kitchen Pickleball

Description: A vibrant online community and podcast, focusing on all things pickleball. It includes forums, tips, and industry news.

Website: www.thekitchenpickleball.com

Meetup Groups

Pickleball Players Meetup

Description: A global platform for organizing local games and events. Many cities have their own pickleball meetup groups.

Website: www.meetup.com/find/?keywords=pickleball

Pickleball Club of America

Description: A meetup group organizing pickleball meetups across various states with a focus on casual play.

Website: www.meetup.com/pickleballclubofamerica

Chapter 25

Online Pickleball Dating Communities

These groups provide a fun way for pickleball enthusiasts to meet others with similar interests and foster connections both on and off the court!

Facebook Groups

Pickleball Singles and Mingles

Description: A group for single pickleball players to meet, chat, and organize casual games or dates.

Website: www.facebook.com/groups/pickleballsinglesmingles

Pickleball Dating Community

Description: A community for single pickleball players looking to connect romantically while enjoying the sport.

Website: www.facebook.com/groups/pickleballdatingcommunity

Pickleball Singles Connection

Description: A space for singles who play pickleball to chat and connect over the sport, with events and game meetups.

Website: www.facebook.com/groups/pickleballsinglesconnection

Meetup Groups

Pickleball Singles Meetup

Description: A Meetup group specifically for pickleball players who are single and interested in meeting others for games and dates.

Website: www.meetup.com/find/?keywords=pickleball+singles

Pickleball and Dating

Description: A group organizing casual pickleball games with a focus on singles meeting and mingling.

Website: www.meetup.com/pickleball-and-dating

ENGAGE WITH ESRA OZ

I would like to thank all of you for purchasing my book. I would love to hear from you on how you experienced *"Pickleball Dating: Love on the Court."* If you are wanting to go deeper in your courageous work in dating, you can find my *Dating Funnel for Women: How to Spot Bad Boys and Filter them out Quickly: 100 Types of Men to Avoid* on Amazon. This is an easy- to-follow guide on identifying and avoiding the types of men who are not worth your time. It teaches a simplistic dating approach, going on multiple dates with a variety of men and filtering out the high-value one, who is offering you the solidity, maturity, and adulthood you need for life partnership.

You can also join my social media community **"Dating Funnel for Women"** on Facebook and/or Instagram. Look for tips on dating and how to create a dating funnel. I look forward to having you join me.

Dating Funnel for Women Podcast

For more tips on how to date with more intention and less stress, listen to my podcast **"Dating Funnel for Women"** on Spotify and Apple Podcast. I also offer live group coaching on a rotating schedule and 1:1 coaching. Check out the website **www.datingfunnelforwomen.com** to see when the next session begins, explore the master class, and download a dating funnel blueprint as a reference for your dating journey and follow me on Instagram **@datingfunnelforwomen** and **@dresraoz**.

www.esraozdenerol.com

www.datingfunnelforwomen.com